Dancing with Divinity:

POSITIVE AFFIRMATIONS FOR ANY SITUATION

DEANNA REITER

This book and accompanying compact disc is available at
special quantity discounts for bulk purchases for sales
promotions, premiums or fund raising. Special books or
book excerpts can also be created to fit specific needs. For
details, please contact the author through her website:
www.dayawati.com.

The information in this book and compact disc is not
designed to replace medical advice and is used at the
reader's discretion.

Text design and typography by Joel van Valin.

FIRST PRINTING 2007

ISBN: 978-0-9800375-0-0

Dancing with Divinity

The music has been playing
since before we have been

The energy has been flowing
since before we have been

The truth is never hidden
although we imagine it has been

And now is the time
for the shift to begin

No matter what the perception
or the belief

Now is the time
to simplify the soul

And stride toward the bliss
that is our birthright

For the echoes of laughter
ring clear

The emancipation of our true selves
is near

And now we can discover
what we have always known

On the purest,
deepest level

That when the music is audible
we shall begin
Dancing with Divinity.

-DR
23 May 2007

Table of Contents

B

C

M

N

T

U

V

W

Introduction

I am intelligent. I am strong. I am confident. I am creative. I enjoy meeting new people. I can accomplish whatever I set my mind to. I am lovable. I love myself. People respect me. I am healthy, happy and whole. I deserve to be happy. I have all that I need.

How many of the above sentences are true for you? Can you look at yourself in the mirror, with direct eye contact, and say them all? Do you believe all of them?

No matter what your belief system or religious background, I invite you to be open to the idea that positive thinking and positive affirmations can enhance your life tremendously.

As your positive thinking expands, you discover that golden opportunities surround you all the time. Opportunities have always been present in your life, whether you have recognized them or not. With this book, you now have an opportunity to harness more favorable experiences into your life. There are many good things in you and in the world. Sometimes we just need to be reminded of them. Think of these positive affirmations as a collection of reminders of all the good around you. Now is the perfect time to deal with every situation as it comes to you with an open heart and an open mind.

As your thinking changes, your perception changes. Thoughts are made of energy. The more positive thoughts we have, the more positive energy we create. More positive energy means more beauty and abundance in the world.

Dancing with Divinity provides you with hundreds of negative emotions you may experience in your daily life.

Instead of drowning in your emotion, take a moment and look up that emotion in this book and read the corresponding positive affirmations. Say them, write them, dance around and shout them. Feel how differently your perspective is once you take away the negative focus and make it positive. With that simple change in perspective, things will change in your life for the better.

Keep your mind open so that you can enhance your thinking positively. There is nothing to lose except your negative energy, negative emotions and negative perception. If you're ready to release all that isn't working in your life, you're ready to use positive affirmations for any situation.

Discover how to begin *Dancing with Divinity*.

Positive Affirmations Explained

Thoughts have a great deal of power and control over the body. Thoughts can dictate your mood, your ability, your physical well being and how you relate to yourself and other people. Your thoughts can alter your perception, your atmosphere, your circumstances and your reality. Positive thinking produces positive results. It enhances the energy around you and affects the people with whom you come in contact. Positive thinking leads to a good perception about the world around you, reducing stress and increasing harmony. Positive affirmations help your self-esteem soar.

Positive affirmations channel our thoughts from habitual, negative patterns that do not benefit our lives in any manner to a place of fuller realization, helping us to reach our true potential. Positive affirmations allow us to gain self acceptance and self love. They reduce the negativity surrounding us and open our mind to infinite possibility.

Think about elite athletes. They spend hours before their competitions visualizing perfect performances. They believe they will succeed. They have an abundance of skill combined with a positive mental belief in their skills. It is that unwavering positive frame of mind that separates fair athletes from superb ones.

Many entrepreneurs and adventure seekers also have this frame of mind. It is that positive mental edge that can make the difference in anyone's daily life. If you wake up believing you will have a great day, you will have a great day because your mind has set that intent for the Universe to fulfill. Once you have consciously decided to have a great day, everything and everyone in your world aligns to fulfill your intent.

Positive affirmations help us to attain a higher consciousness of what it is we desire from ourselves and from the world around us. Positive affirmations are not meant to control others in a negative way. They also do not create miracles from something totally implausible. For example, repeating a positive affirmation that you will receive delicious honey from a cow or milk from a beehive would be a wasted effort.

Focus on positive affirmations that are probable even if you don't know how they will evolve. Trust that the outcome that is in your best interest is already occurring and then detach from the outcome. Leave it up to the Universe to figure out how it will happen. In the meantime, pay attention to what things you are being drawn to and signs that are leading you in a certain direction. Be willing to say yes to golden opportunities that magically bring you toward your greatest desires.

Get Conscious by Examining Your Thoughts

The rapid pace of our minds is astounding. Approximately fifty thousand thoughts float through our heads each day. Fifty-thousand! The task of staying conscious with this many daily thoughts is daunting, but begin by getting conscious on just a few thoughts each day. The thoughts that you want to pay attention to are the negative thoughts, such as: "It's too hot. I'm tired. I'm hungry. I'm bored. I'm not smart enough. I'm not good enough. I'm wrong. I'm bad." Statements such as these are the ones you want to recognize, release and replace.

Of all your negative thoughts, the most dominant one is the one you need to eradicate. This is your core negative belief. It is this belief that is predominantly keeping you from attaining everything that you truly desire in your life. To discover this core negative belief, write on a sheet of paper: "My core negative beliefs." Then write the words: "I am" and complete the sentence with the first five negative thoughts that spring into your mind.

You may write: "I am not trustworthy. I am stupid. I am always wrong. I am bad. I am incapable." After you write five negatives, write: "The most appalling thought I have about myself is: I am ____." This may be one of your first five negative core beliefs or it may be a new one. Complete the statement with the first thing that comes into your mind. Do not take a long time to think about your answer. Any answer you write is acceptable, except "I don't know." In reality, you *do* know, but you think it may be safer to avoid discovering it. If this is the case, that's okay. You could skip this section until a later date when you are more open to discovering your core negative belief. Simply work on positive affirmations until that time and be sure that you hold yourself accountable to returning to this section.

After you have completed the sentence and unearthed this core negative belief, the next step is to take that belief and make it positive. If your thought is: "I am always wrong" change it to: "Everything I do is right for me" or "I make the right decisions for me." If neither of these statements resonates with you, pick a positive affirmation from the situation: "When You're Feeling Like You're Always Wrong" or write your own.

When I began working with positive affirmations, I recognized there were still areas of my life that I was limiting myself from receiving my truest desires. No matter how much I repeated my positive affirmations, I was still blocked. I knew there was some core negative belief I needed to release to allow the positive thoughts their space. I noticed that I had been creating small accidents in my life where I was physically causing myself pain, like stubbing my toe. I wanted to be clear about what thought I was holding on to when I hurt myself, no matter how minor the incident. So every time I stubbed my toe or bumped into something, I stopped what I was doing and examined the thought I was having.

I remember one morning I returned to bed to find my cat sprawled out in the spot in which I had been sleeping. I hit my shin on the edge of the bed frame and screamed in pain. As I examined my bloody shin, I also examined my thoughts. What had I been thinking when I hurt myself? My dominant negative thought had been: "My cat can sleep anywhere on the bed. Why does she have to steal my spot?" This is a thought of limitation and lack. Ultimately, the thought stemmed from the belief that "things are stolen from me" and from the core negative belief that "I don't get my fair share." The incident reminded me of times in my childhood when I had left my chair to do something and my spot was "stolen," forcing me to find another place to sit. It also reminded me of other things that had been taken from me as a child. That belief led me to guard my possessions at all times. I grew up feeling like I had to watch my back. I made people earn my trust.

Over the years I realized that by replacing my fear of lack with positive thinking, I attracted good things to me. By trusting that human nature is good, I did not have to be a security guard with my things anymore. However, my cat made me aware that the belief had not totally been eradicated. That morning when I hit my shin on the corner of the bed, I realized that I was still more focused on what I didn't have rather than what I did have. I still had a fear of lack. Half of my queen size bed was available to me, yet I only cared about the small space that my cat was occupying.

A few weeks later, I scraped the bottom of a door frame against my foot causing another bloody gash. Recovering from the pain, I retraced my thoughts and realized that I was thinking about not being fairly compensated for a class I had taught. Once again, the belief that I didn't get my fair share returned.

In each situation, I recognized that I needed to clean up the aftermath of the incident physically and mentally. I washed away the blood and then began to wash away the negative belief. I thanked the Universe for the clear wake-up calls regarding my negative thinking. Every day, I affirmed: "Knowing that we are all one, I want what is best for me and what is best for other people. I have an abundance of everything that allows me to share with others. There is enough for everyone, including me."

Pain is a physical manifestation of your mind's negative thoughts, thoughts that focus on the past or the future and thoughts that negate your highest good or life path. It is possible to live a pain-free life, you only need to have a mind full of positive, present and highly vibrating thoughts. Notice when you are unhappy or when things are not going right in your life. Ask yourself what thought you are holding onto that is creating this less than perfect manifestation for yourself. Accept whatever answer(s) come your way, except "I don't know." Recognize how those thoughts may have helped you in the past.

For example, holding on to the negative belief that "I don't get my fair share" allows me to have something to complain about. Based on my past experiences, I know that others will console me if I have a complaint. It also allows me to depend on others more and therefore others won't depend on me. It helps me to feel a little helpless rather than become fully responsible in the world. That means I can have more fun and be like a kid. My fair share might actually overwhelm me. I probably wouldn't know what to do if I got my fair share. That would be scary for me. These are some of the many reasons why I chose to stay stuck in this core negative belief and why so many others are stuck with the same belief.

After recognizing the core negative belief and why you hold on to that belief, release it and replace it. Transform the negative belief to something positive. When I affirm: "I have an abundance of everything that allows me to share with others," I may notice the following negative responses arise: "It is scary to share with others. Other people don't appreciate what I have to share with them. People will become dependent on me if I give them things. Being a responsible adult is boring." (The Negative Response Technique (NRT) is explained in greater detail later in this book.) Recognizing these negative responses, I see that it would be beneficial for me to also affirm: "It is safe for me to share with others. Other people enjoy reaping in the abundance that I share with them. Being a mature and responsible adult is fun and easy. There is a perfect balance of independence and dependence in my world."

A friend of mine who was in massage school told me he was unhappy because he wasn't receiving any compliments or any good tips from his clients. Knowing that he is a good massage therapist, I knew he must have some negative thought, such as "I'm not good enough," rooted in his core that prevented him from receiving compliments and tips. I suggested he use the affirmation: "I deserve love and praise."

He used the affirmation the next day and received a twenty dollar tip from a client and positive feedback from one of his instructors. He was elated that the affirmation had worked. However, despite the positive results from his affirmation, he stopped using it. He allowed his core negative belief to prevail. His self approval and self love was at a level where he refused to believe that he was deserving of love and praise. He continued to receive terrible tips and little positive feedback. In fact, during one massage, he got his wallet stolen! He had returned to his former comfort level of complaining about not receiving what he wanted rather than stretch himself to believe that he truly was worthy to receive all that he wanted. He continues to work on his self love and self approval and has been more receptive to slower and safer manifestations of love and praise.

The only limitation to this process is your mind and your willingness. Enjoy the practice of weeding out your negative thoughts and benefiting in the beautiful life you manifest with your positive thoughts.

Tips for Positive Affirmations

Use positive language

Positive wording in your affirmations carries much more power than negative words. Avoid words such as not, no, don't, etc. Although it seems obvious, negative words have a tendency to slip into our unconscious minds and into our language without recognizing they are negative. When someone says that he is doing "not too bad," there is implied language that he is not doing well either. Someone who says, "I see no reason why I can't make this work" also implies that she sees no reason why she *can* make it work. Someone who asks, "Why don't we go on a picnic?" is asking for a reason why they shouldn't go rather than why they should.

By saying, "I'm doing well," we affirm how well we are doing. By saying, "I can make this work," we show confidence in our abilities. By saying, "Let's go on a picnic," we bring enthusiasm toward our invitation.

So it is with positive affirmations. Rather than affirming: "I am not scared to speak in front of a large audience," affirm: "I am confident of my voice and my abilities in the presence of others."

There are times when I specifically use "not" or "no" in affirmations. For example, "It is not my business what others think of me" and "I choose to no longer remain in situations in my life that are less than ideal." Both phrases can easily be made positive, however I have kept the statements exactly as they are because it is important to acknowledge and release what *isn't* working in your life, so that you can *then* bring in what is right for you.

After you have worked with the affirmation for a certain amount of time that seems appropriate for you, you can alter the affirmations to become completely positive. The above affirmations could then be changed to, "Everyone in my world accepts me for who I am" or "Every situation in my life is ideal for me." I recommend that you sculpt your affirmations until they are a perfect fit for you. Your focal affirmations could change hourly or they could remain the same for years. Each person is different, with different situations and different perceptions of those situations. Be open and flexible with what is working best for you at any given moment.

With few exceptions, the affirmations in this book are stated positively. My suggestion for you is to get rid of the negative words and the negative energy. Test it out with your body by saying the affirmation with the negative word and then without it. For example, "I no longer need to worry about what the future holds for me" can be changed to "The future holds good things for me." To me, the second affirmation resonates much better in my body and uplifts my spirit. "There's nothing keeping me from success" can be changed to "I am successful." Again, I feel better with the second affirmation than the first. It leaves me smiling and secure, ready to move forward with confidence and grace.

Use present tense

Affirmations are most effective in the present tense, as if you believe they're happening right now. For example, the affirmation: "I will communicate one hundred percent from my heart and soul" would become: "I communicate one hundred percent from my heart and soul." The word "will" denotes the future and that someday it will happen. But there is no telling when someday will come. It could be thirty days from now or thirty years from now. There is little immediacy in using future tense. The Universe will pick up on your lack of urgency and ultimately in your lack of belief in your affirmation. Eliminating "will" brings the affirmation alive today. I would much rather communicate effectively today than wait until someday to be a good communicator.

Tomorrow is always tomorrow. It remains ahead of us. Today is always today. It is always in the here and now. The advertising industry follows this same principle, with messages such as, 'treat yourself *today*' or 'call *now* to take advantage of this *limited time* offer.' Notice that they don't suggest that 'you treat yourself *tomorrow*' or that you can 'call *later* to take advantage of a never ending offer.' If they tell their customers to wait until tomorrow or to call later, they'll be missing out on millions of customers *all the time*.

Your most present thoughts and actions will bring about your greatest gains. The advertising industry sends out its messages to the Universe in present tense and that is what gets it the greatest results. The same is true for you sending out your thoughts and words to the Universe. Keep your affirmations alive with the energy of the present moment.

Use strong language

Use the strongest language possible to harness the greatest amount of energy to your affirmation. As much as possible, try to eliminate the words: "have to," "should," "try," "can't" and "I don't know" from your vocabulary. They are disempowering words that detach you from the process of creating your reality. The words: "have to" removes you from gratitude. It keeps you confined to an obligation rather than becoming conscious that you have a choice. "Should" removes your desire. The words: "try," "can't" and "I don't know" remove you from belief. Remove the words and remove the blocks they carry.

For example, the affirmation: "I try to live ethically and morally" can be changed to: "I live ethically and morally." The affirmation: "I am good enough" can be changed to: "I am magnificent." The affirmation: "I have plenty of time" can become: "I have all the time I need to do all that I need to do." When you say an affirmation and it does not inspire you or energize you, check to see if you are using the strongest words to carry your message effectively to the Universe. Remove the weak words and make your affirmations powerful.

Do not suppress negative emotions

Don't hold back your feelings, positive or negative. Take the opportunity and recognize what it is you are feeling as you experience a situation. Allow yourself to move through your emotions. When we suppress emotions, we leave our physical body no choice but to retain that emotion inside of us. That negative emotion becomes toxic to our bodies. These toxins can cause physical ailments.

Once you are aware of your emotion, recognize why it is present. Are you feeling angry? Why? Is it because someone crossed your boundary? Did someone say or do something that violated you? Did you do something that was self sabotaging? Figure out the cause of your anger.

Once you've identified the correlation between the cause and the emotion, you can then move through the emotion. Use the positive affirmations to help you do this. Review the section on Getting Conscious with your Thoughts to maneuver through this process more deeply.

Take action

Positive affirmations work well when we put our physical energy behind them. There are times when we need to take steps to manifest our goals and dreams. For example, when you're feeling disgusted, let's say because your house is a mess, don't simply turn to the positive affirmations for feeling disgusted and will your house to be clean. Get up and clean your house, pay someone to clean it or ask your friends or family to help you clean it. Take a step toward making it the cozy, relaxing home that you love.

If the task before you seems daunting, examine why you are intimidated or overwhelmed. Get to the root of the problem. Is your house messy because you're lacking time or energy to clean it? Are you depressed or unmotivated? Then look to positive affirmations to help you through those issues.

We need to be willing to say and do the things that we feel inspired to do. We may not feel one hundred percent confident about doing them, but we know that we will benefit by doing them. The world around us will benefit, too. Sometimes those things may force us out of our comfort zones. Sometimes they might increase our heart rates or make us sweat a bit. Our stomachs might flip and our hands might shake, but deep inside us we know that taking that step is for our highest good. Taking that step will move us forward on our paths.

The intuitive voice inside each of us may not leave us alone until we take action. When our intuition tells us to initiate a conversation with that beautiful stranger on the bus or to apply for a position we're not quite qualified for, we need to take those risks. We can't sit back and hide behind positive affirmations to find the perfect mate or the perfect job while refusing to do the things to carry the affirmations forward. Using affirmations without action is like riding a bike with a rusty chain. It is inefficient and foolish.

Do not override your intuition. If you know you need to act in order to adequately move through a situation, don't simply repeat positive affirmations. Get up and take action!

Listen to a recording of affirmations

Listening to a recording of positive affirmations is a highly effective technique. You can either listen to the *Dancing with Divinity* compact disc or you can make a recording of yourself and choose affirmations specific to you. You can record yourself saying the affirmations or you can record someone else's voice. Play the affirmations when they can captivate your full attention, like when you are falling asleep at night.

Speak affirmations with conviction

Stand in front of the mirror and say them to yourself or look a good friend in the eyes and tell them your affirmation. Be sure you articulate your words and speak them with confidence and love. A monotone or slurred affirmation carries much less energy than one said clearly with enthusiasm. Get fired up about your affirmations. Proclaim them with passion. Broadcast them with belief. Communicate them with courage.

Use the first, second and third person

You can also do affirmations in the first, second and third person along with your name. For example, the affirmation: "I deserve to be happy" would become: "I,

Jason, deserve to be happy. He, Jason, deserves to be happy. You, Jason, deserve to be happy." Personalizing your affirmation with your name brings a greater sense of ownership and using the second and third person triggers different reactions than saying it in the first person does.

Remain detached from the outcome

Having goals and desires is human. Many times we act with a specific outcome in mind. As much as you are conscious and able, avoid focusing on outcomes. Do the right thing that feels right for you in the moment. Have faith in the Universe that you will be taken care of and that your desires will be met. Remember that we can only see a small part of the bigger picture. What seems like something so perfect for us at the time can have dire consequences down the line. The section on The Highest Good goes into greater detail on this subject.

Experiment and be creative

The positive affirmations that are provided in this book are a perfect starting point to bring awareness to your emotional states and your body. You then can take the steps to change the negativity in your life.

Affirmations can be spoken, meditated upon, written, sung, shouted, painted or conveyed through any other creative medium. You can focus on your affirmations while walking, driving, swimming, cooking or writing in a journal. Two of the best times for your mind and body to fully integrate affirmations are before falling asleep and upon waking. You can write your affirmations on a piece of paper and place it on your nightstand, your refrigerator, your dashboard, your bathroom mirror or wherever else you may want to reflect on it.

Recognize that what works well for one person may not work at all for you. An affirmation that works for you in one situation may not work at all for you in another situation, even though you are feeling the same emotion. Experiment and adapt the affirmations to make them right for you. Over time, you may find that varying your affirmation works better for you now than it did before. You may get creative and find a new system altogether.

There is no wrong way to do positive affirmations. The most important thing is that you are doing the affirmations and that you believe in them and the power they have to alter your life and your reality. Your thoughts add to the peace and harmony of the Universe. The more positive your thoughts and your frame of mind, the more peace and harmony flow into the Universe.

To summarize, here are some of the main things to remember when working with positive affirmations:

- Use positive language
- Use present tense
- Use strong language
- Do not suppress negative emotions
- Take action
- Listen to a recording of affirmations
- Speak affirmations with conviction
- Use the first, second and third person
- Remain detached from the outcome
- Experiment and be creative

The Five Treasures

There are five treasures of wisdom we can carry to help us in any situation. These five treasures will not weigh us down nor get in our way. They are not finite. These treasures can be shared by everyone without fear of using them up. These treasures can be called upon time and time again to help us be successful in our lives.

Very simply, here are the five treasures: Recognize that you create your reality, trust the Universe, let your heart lead, be grateful and breathe. They are simple and effective, easy to draw out of our pockets when we need them.

The First Treasure: Reality

Thought is creative. Energy is behind every thought you have. The more beautiful and happy your internal thoughts are, the more beautiful and happy your external environment will be. If you focus on what is not working in your life rather than what is working, you will harness more things to you that aren't working as you'd like them to.

Take a look at your current reality. Do you like where you live? Do you like your job? Your car? Your social life? Are you healthy? Is your family healthy? Are your pets and plants healthy? Is there anything in your house that is broken and needs to be fixed or is everything in good working order? Are you happy? On a scale of one to ten, how satisfied are you with the reality that you've created for yourself?

If you aren't at a ten, what will it take to get you there? What can you do to change your current reality? Positive affirmations can be a huge step toward improving your reality. Getting conscious with your thoughts and your perception will also help. Taking action will shift your life in the direction you want it to go.

You can choose to be happy or choose to be miserable. Your choices may be unconscious or conscious. But recognize that you have control over the choices in your life.

That can be a hard concept to accept. When I first was introduced to it, I understood it to a certain level, yet I couldn't accept some parts of it. For instance, I found myself in a relationship with a man who didn't want to be in a relationship. He initially talked himself into believing he wanted a relationship and later shut down on me completely. We went camping for a weekend and he was non-communicative and slept the majority of the weekend. I was angry at him for shutting down and wanting so much time alone.

I understood that I had manifested a relationship with a man who I put to sleep and who wouldn't communicate with me. I had a hard time accepting that I was responsible for my reaction to him. I was miserable – very sad and angry and lonely. Every feeling I had was my perception and my reality. Yet rather than accept responsibility for my emotions, I blamed him for making me feel terrible.

When I was able to stop blaming him for my misery, I asked myself what thoughts I had that allowed this to happen. I came to understand that I believed it was difficult for me to communicate with men and that I'm not worth their effort when the relationship becomes difficult. Hence, my partner stopped communicating and fell asleep. He was playing his role perfectly in the reality I had established. Likewise, he had some of his own issues to work out and I was playing into his reality as well. Once we both recognized the reality we had created, we were able to change the situation.

Aside from non-functional relationships, it can also be difficult to believe that we create diseases in our body, poor financial situations and bad luck for ourselves. But understanding that every thought, every object and every atom is made up of a vibrating energy brings clarity to the picture. It is your choice if you want to harness good, pure, positive energy around you or if you want to attract negative, stale energy.

When you find yourself creating a reality that you don't like, discover the lesson that results from that experience.

Recognize how you have created your reality. Do not blame anyone else or anything else for your misery. No one else has power over your feelings. On some level, conscious or unconscious, you have manifested everything that comes into your life. When you are persuaded by someone or something, for an action you regret, do not point a finger at anyone else. You are the one who became convinced and you are in control of your actions. You construct your reality. You are responsible for everything that happens to you.

You have created your past and your present. You are creating your future.

Knowing the first treasure empowers you to accept your reality. It also empowers you to change your reality and mold it into what you desire.

The Second Treasure: The Universe

Choose whatever name you like for whatever higher power you feel closest to. It may be God, Allah, Yahweh, Jesus Christ, the Universe, Spirit, a deceased family member, a deceased friend, a guardian angel, a spirit guide or an essence of Spirit or Divinity. Your higher power resides within you and outside of you. Trust in that power. Put your faith in it. Help it to lead you toward your highest good and the highest good of other humans, animals and all objects.

Ask this higher power for energy throughout the day. Ask it for motivation. Ask it to support you and present you with golden opportunities. Talk to your higher power. Spend part of each day listening to your higher power in meditation. Ask to receive clear directions.

There is never a need to be alone, unhappy or lacking anything because there is abundance in the Universe. Tap into that abundance. Don't ignore the possibilities awaiting you.

The Third Treasure: The Heart

The mind is powerful. It likes to take control. The mind is like a bossy big brother who gets to take charge even though he's not best suited for the job. Along with our minds, we are led by our stomachs, our eyes, our sexual organs, our noses, our ears and our egos.

No matter what decision you face, ask your heart what it wants to do. Ask for the solution for your highest good and the highest good of everyone involved. Don't make a decision based on money, greed, sexual pleasure or status. Make your choices with compassion.

The head, and the ego, like to get involved. Let them have their say, take their opinions into consideration and then ask your heart for the best solution. Check in with your higher power as well. When you allow your heart and your higher power to become your masters, you will be led in a direction that serves your higher purpose.

Imagine you are faced with an opportunity to be Vice President of the XYZ group you belong to. Your heart does not want to accept the position, but you feel a sense of obligation to your friend who has accepted the

Presidency and wants you to be her VP. If your heart doesn't want to be VP, listen to it. Truthfully, your friend would rather have someone who wants to be a VP rather than someone who lacks energy and motivation for the position. There is a better person out there for the job and you don't want to stand in the way of him or her.

One of the biggest fights we have with ourselves is between our head and our hearts. Who is stuck in the middle, forced to mediate? Our throats. Physical ailments can result because of this ongoing struggle. For example, millions of people currently have issues with their thyroid, many of which are undiagnosed, because we fight between our head and our heart with the throat left as the battle ground. Our will is connected to the energy of our throats. By continually trampling down your will, you put the thyroid and other glands and organs in your throat at risk.

Why allow this internal fight? Instead, allow the solution to present itself. Check in with your heart to be sure it's a solution that uplifts you. When you're accepting an invitation, planning what you're going to say to someone or even contemplating what to eat, listen to your heart. Make sure what you're about to do is going to bring you more peace and joy. If it won't, then don't do it. If the consequences for not doing something are going to bring you misery, weigh your options with your heart and make the better choice.

Say and do everything with your heart in command. When you need to be in charge of something, let your heart be in charge. No matter what comes up, if you look to your heart, it will respond with a fair and compassionate answer.

The Fourth Treasure: Gratitude

Appreciate all that you receive. There is a purpose to everything and a reason why everything happens exactly as it does. Recognize the synchronicity in things unfolding around you and be grateful that such wonderful things can occur. I often rejoice when I see or smell a beautiful flower and when there are beautiful clouds dancing in the sky. I take pleasure in little things like this. I rejoice that I have good vision to enjoy the clouds and a good sense of smell to appreciate the flower.

Although I spend a great deal of my time in gratitude, I know I am not able to express it one hundred percent of the time. So, instead I thank the Universe for everything that has been given to me and everything that is being prepared for me. This blanket appreciation helps to cover all the things I miss.

Volunteering and making a difference in other people's lives is a great way to actively show the Universe your appreciation for your talents. It also gives you an opportunity to share your talents with others. Many volunteer positions quickly remind you of how fortunate you are. There are a number of situations where people are in need of support from their community, such as a homeless shelter, a food kitchen, a nursing home, a hospital or an impoverished community. It's difficult to complain about not having enough money to upgrade your speedboat when you are writing a letter for someone who had his arm amputated. It's equally awkward to dwell on having stained your favorite pants when you're helping someone who only owns one pair of pants that are in much worse shape than yours.

Do not feel bad about your good fortune, but take the time to recognize how blessed you are. Appreciate the reality you have created for yourself. Share your time, talents and prosperity with others when you are willing and able to do so.

Another great way to show the Universe your appreciation for all that you have received, is to make a daily list of ten things for which you are grateful. Take a moment upon waking or before sleeping to write this list and reflect on your day. Gratitude at any time of day is a simple way to uplift your spirits.

Be grateful for your friends and your acquaintances. Appreciate good health, a good memory, the ability to read, to breathe and to walk. Be thankful that you can eat, think, create, sing, help others and smile.

Be grateful for life. Be grateful for love. Be grateful for all the abundance in the Universe.

The Fifth Treasure: The Breath

As babies, we breathe in a full, connected rhythm. It is a peaceful rhythm, one that allows complete circulation in our small bodies. It is untainted by our environment and unhampered by our emotions. It is unaffected by gravity, poor posture or bad habits. It is Divine.

Soon enough, that rhythm changes. Think about the last time you were anxious, scared or angry. Most likely, you held your breath. You stopped the continual flow of Divine energy from circulating within your soul. Think about the last time you were depressed or tired. Perhaps you began to breathe more shallowly, feeling as though you didn't have the energy to breathe fully and deeply. Again, you denied yourself from your connection to the Universe.

Allow your breath to expand in your diaphragm as you inhale. Then allow the air to expand laterally into your ribcage. Lastly, let the air rise up into your chest, filling it with oxygen. As you exhale, allow the air to first leave your chest, then your ribcage and finally your belly, contracting each area as the air is pushed out of it. Take ten full breaths, moving the air in a circular rhythm without a pause at the top of the inhalation nor at the bottom of the exhalation. Notice how your body feels. Are you tingling at all? Do you feel calmer? More peaceful?

Breathing fully and deeply changes the pH level of the blood, lowers the blood pressure and minimizes perceived stress in the body. By taking ten deep breaths, you create the space to slow your mind and listen to your intuition, which helps you to make sound decisions. You also avoid saying or doing something rash.

A few deep breaths help us act more clearly. Consciously breathe when you are distressed or under intense pressure. Your reaction will be far different than it otherwise would be.

These five treasures, when combined with positive affirmations, will bring ease and clarity to any situation.

Here is a summary of the five treasures:

- Recognize how you are creating your reality
- Tap into the Universe
- Let your heart lead
- Be grateful
- Breathe

The Highest Good

Many of the affirmations in this book include the words "highest good." This refers to the highest good of the self and may also include the highest good of everyone involved. It is important that these words are in the affirmation to remind us that the realization of our intent and desire should be considered with the effect that they will have on our lives and on the lives of others.

When we allow our heart to lead (one of the five treasures of wisdom), we take the first step to ensure that something is for our highest good, however we do not want our affirmations to conflict with the Universe's plan. Making a decision from the heart with the highest good for everyone brings the best outcome.

For example, say you are writing an affirmation that you will get a promotion at work. (In present tense, this affirmation would be something like: "I am the new team manager at XYZ Group.") You want the promotion because it pays more, gives you a greater challenge, and offers you more prestige. However, what you are not aware of is that getting the promotion at this time would mean longer hours at work and this would ultimately cause a huge strain on your marriage and family life. This would result in a great deal of anguish on you, your spouse, your dog and your two year-old son. It is possible that a divorce would result.

Another employee under consideration for the job is a single woman whose mother recently died and left behind a mountain of debt. Equally qualified for the promotion, it is clear that she would benefit a great deal from the position, while you and your family would suffer. With this inside view, you clearly recognize that you wouldn't want the promotion after all. It would be better to remove your will from the affirmation and re-state it: "I am the new team manager at XYZ Group, if it is for my highest good and the highest good of everyone involved."

The highest good (or the worst consequences) may not be known to you. In the example above, you are not aware of the possibility that divorce may result due to the longer hours that come with your promotion. You are only aware that your positive affirmation did not work. Trust that not receiving the outcome of your affirmation is for your highest good. Believe that when something you desire does not work out for you, something better is coming. Instead of getting the promotion as team manager, you may get a better position at a different company with more family-friendly work policies.

Whether or not you say or write the entire affirmation with the new addendum, be sure that your intent with any affirmation is that it is for the highest good of all involved.

Perception

Along with positive thinking, perception is an important component for a peaceful, comfortable life. You can recognize the "good" in things or the "bad" in things. It's your choice how you decide to perceive things. And it is this perception that is responsible for your stress level. That means that *you* create the stress in your body. It is not your boss, your children, your spouse, the traffic, the neighbor, the news, the state of the environment or the president. It is how you perceive and react to these things that determine your stress.

Appreciate the "good" as well as the "bad." Sometimes, the things we perceive to be bad are actually better than the things we perceive as good and vice versa. Many people often perceive the end of a relationship to be a bad thing. They are miserable and depressed and a few horrible thoughts about themselves or their former partner arise. They may think they wasted their time. They may believe that it was another failed relationship. But in actuality, there is no such thing as a failed relationship. We learn a great deal from other people, especially those to whom we are close. Every relationship is successful for teaching us or healing us – whether we recognize it or not. The same goes for a failed business or unachieved goal. Each failure could be seen as a great success if we learn the lesson we are given. When someone or something leaves our lives, it merely clears the space for an even more magical and special new person or thing to enter.

A friend of mine found himself late for work one morning. He was driving above the speed limit to make up for his tardiness. He began cursing at every slow driver and every red light. And then in the middle of his commute, he witnessed the aftermath of a horrible accident involving several vehicles. An ambulance was already at the scene and someone was being carried on a stretcher. He recognized that if he had been on time that day, he quite possibly could have been the one on that stretcher. He grew calm and drove more carefully even though it meant he would arrive later. Grateful that he was safe, he recognized his tardiness as a "good" thing.

Watch how you perceive whatever situation you encounter. You can go to the bank every other Friday afternoon and find yourself waiting in a long line. You can be angry and resentful during your wait, cursing under your breath that the bank should hire more tellers. You can purse your lips and furl your brow, set your hands on your hips and tap your foot impatiently. Or you can enjoy the time you are waiting in line by chatting to the person next to you. You could do any number of other things to occupy yourself. It's your choice if you want to be happy or miserable. Either way, you'll be waiting in line.

If you are truly displeased with the service at the bank on Fridays, choose another day to go to the bank. Or choose another bank. Or tell a manager at the bank that you are unhappy with the service you receive and you'd like more tellers hired. Take a step to resolve your misery by changing your perception of the situation or by taking action. Since you are the only one responsible for yourself and your body, if you are unhappy with your reality, it is up to you to change it.

Trust in the Universe that you are always led in the right direction that is for your highest good and the highest good of others. Discover the lessons that arise. Find the benefit in every situation and know with complete confidence that there is always a benefit. Some of the greatest inventions were created because of absolute disasters. Let your "disasters" be spectacular events in your life. Release unnecessary stress from your body by believing that you are a magnet for all things good. And then find that good in everything and everyone – every single day.

Shedding Doubt

If there is a shred of doubt in any of your affirmations, the Universe responds to your doubt. For example, instead of waking up saying, "Today's going to be a great day!" you might find yourself saying, "I hope today is better than yesterday" or "I'm going to try to have a good day." Neither of these statements is powerful. Likewise, saying something such as, "I'm going to have a great day, as long as I don't have that meeting with my boss," also harnesses energy toward having a less than perfect day. The perfect day does not reach quite a zenith of perfection because the dreaded possibility of a meeting lurks around every corner. There is a part of you that dwells on that possibility and even the thought of an uncomfortable meeting with your boss throws off your entire day, whether the meeting occurs or not. If potential sabotage exists, the ideal is marred.

Why not wake up saying, "Today is a great day!" Ultimately, any of the other statements lead you toward self-sabotage. Focus your energy on everything about your day being great rather than it being better than yesterday or "trying" to have a good day. Do not set up any caveats for possible limitations of a great day.

Given the choice of hosting an outdoor party in June on a day with a sixty-five percent chance of rain or a five percent chance of rain, most people would choose the day with the five percent chance of rain. Who wants to have a party when there are black clouds looming overhead and rain pending every moment? It is much more enjoyable to be at an outdoor party with blue skies, knowing with ninety-five percent certainty that it will stay sunny and clear.

That analogy works the same way with the energy of the Universe. When you believe in something completely and release all doubts, you manifest your best reality.

Whether you are creating a perfect day, emotional stability, more freedom in your life, improved relationships, better health or any number of other things, positive affirmations help you on your journey most effectively when doubts are diminished.

Identify and erase any disbelief associated with your affirmation. Even the tiniest bit of doubt may attract an unwanted result. It only takes one drop of blood to attract a shark. So it is with doubt. If it surfaces, recognize it and release it. Continue to recognize and release your doubt until you believe in your affirmation and it becomes a part of you. Allowing doubt to fester only attracts "sharks."

The Negative Response Technique in the next section will help you release doubt or disbelief about your affirmation.

The Negative Response Technique

The process of shedding doubt related to an affirmation is called The Negative Response Technique. If you consider an affirmation to be truly outrageous, or perhaps even a lie, your internal doubt or Negative Response (NR) is high. Take for instance, the affirmation: "People enjoy being around me." Each time you say this affirmation, you may have a different NR. You may first think: "If people enjoyed being around me, then why am I always by myself?" The next time, you may think: "Nobody enjoys being around me! I never get invited to anything." Other responses you might have are: "I wasn't given enough attention as I child and I still don't get enough attention as an adult. If people enjoyed being around me, why am I home alone on Friday night? Am I introverted because that's my nature, or have I convinced myself that I'm introverted because I grew up lonely? People would rather be around someone funnier than me."

The NRs may continue for weeks, perhaps even after saying the affirmation more than one hundred or one thousand times. Eventually, your thinking shifts. Your NRs will be silenced as your doubt lessens. You will have grown tired arguing with yourself. You will stop wrestling with your inner critic and you'll start to hear things such as: "I guess some people enjoy being around me. Well I do tell pretty entertaining stories. Come to think of it, last time I was at a party, I was the center of attention for a while. Maybe people do enjoy being around me."

Sooner or later, you allow your mind to realize with greater confidence that yes, people enjoy being around you. And once you grasp that concept, you begin to find more people in your circle of friends, more invitations on Friday nights and more wanted attention. In turn, once you realize that people do, in fact, enjoy being around you, the affirmation is easier to say. The reality becomes established over time.

By working with positive affirmations, you are squashing that critical, judgmental voice inside you that tells you that you cannot do something or that you're not as good as someone else. With some affirmations, you may at first feel as though you are lying to yourself. One of my clients had the affirmation: "I am beautiful." Indeed she was and sporadically her friends confirmed her affirmation, but she refused to believe their words. To her, they were lies. She thought her friends were only trying to boost her self-esteem. Every time she said her affirmation, she also thought she was lying. She hated the affirmation and wanted to stop using it.

Growing up, her father had never told her she was pretty. For that matter, neither had her mother, a former beauty queen, but it had been her father's approval and the approval of other men in her life that she had been seeking. Her father had never complimented her beauty and she had therefore believed that men didn't find her attractive. Yet she committed to saying the affirmation. Little by little, she became more comfortable with it and her confidence grew. She began dating a lovely, genuine man, who helped her recognize her beauty in a much deeper level than she had ever been able to acknowledge. The NRs and the "lies" gradually diminished.

When you devote your energy to an affirmation, the Universe works with you in creating your new reality. Keep in mind that a subconscious lie that you've been telling yourself for decades may take time to undo. Of course, don't dismiss the idea of spontaneous reprogramming with affirmations, but if your results are not immediate, don't be discouraged. A few days, months or years spent reprogramming something that took decades to solidify is a fairly good deal.

One affirmation I had a difficult time believing was: "Men are safe and always want what is best for me." I had been through a series of bad relationships and had come to a point where I realized I was alienating men from my life and swearing off intimate relationships. Finally, one morning I wrote a list of ten men in my life who had always been gentle and calm in my presence. I had never heard any of them raise their voices. They were easy-going, humorous, supportive men who offered their help to others willingly. I meditated on these ten men, focusing on specific times they were kind to me, until I was so full of their softness and love that I could extend their gentle nature to all the men in my life.

I continued repeating the affirmation for the next several weeks. The next time I wrote out my list of safe men, I realized that all the men in my life were safe and loving toward me. They wanted the best for me and I was ready to accept only the best from them. Soon afterward, I altered the affirmation to: "Everyone in my life is safe and always wants what's best for me." It was equally successful. Every man, woman, and child that entered my life was there to honor my highest good as well as their own.

With the Universe's help, I recognized and allowed people into my life that served my highest good and I was only allowed into their lives when I could serve their highest good. If I felt in any way that the encounter was negative, I removed myself from the other person or group. Often times, the exit was not a conscious one. The affirmation effortlessly worked for me.

A Closer Look at the Negative Response Technique

If you choose a positive affirmation that carries a Negative Response (NR) for you, identify the NR that is elicited. Write it down. It is useful to see the NR pattern unfold. This gives a physical representation of the healing process of your mind. It may also get you to realize what events in your life became stumbling blocks for other situations. Healing that one event can create a snowball effect and help to heal several other issues in your present and your future.

You can also alter your affirmation by taking your NR and turning it into a positive affirmation. Sometimes, the positive affirmation that results is the same as your original affirmation, but in many cases it becomes an entirely new affirmation. These new affirmations may be more personal and relevant to you than your initial affirmation and you may want to focus on the new affirmation instead.

We can see how this works with the affirmation: "People enjoy being around me."

NR: If people enjoyed being around me, then why am I always by myself?
New Affirmation: I am surrounded by people who care about me.

NR: Nobody enjoys being around me! I never get invited to anything.
New Affirmation: Everybody enjoys being around me. I am invited to everything.

NR: I wasn't given enough attention as I child and I still don't get enough as an adult.
New Affirmation: I deserve and enjoy receiving attention.

NR: If people enjoyed being around me, why am I home alone on Friday night?
New Affirmation: My Friday evenings are spent with others.

NR: Am I introverted because that's my nature, or is it a result of growing up lonely?
New Affirmation: I am free to choose when I want to be introverted or extroverted.

NR: People would rather be around someone funnier than me.
New Affirmation: People enjoy my sense of humor and choose to be around me.

You may realize that your pulse quickens most with the new affirmation: "I deserve and enjoy receiving attention." You can add it onto your old affirmation: "People enjoy being around me. I deserve and enjoy receiving attention." Or you can focus on the new affirmation: "I deserve and enjoy receiving attention." Choose the affirmation that really hits a nerve for you. It could be a statement that you have difficulty reading, one that finds you short of breath or one that triggers a memory. Essentially, it may be a statement that says, "Aha! That's exactly the sort of thing I need to start believing about myself!"

Be aware of where in your body you feel tension arise as you say the affirmation. For instance, you may feel your throat tighten when you repeat, "People enjoy being around me." Because the throat is the communication center (please see the Appendix for further explanation), the thought of others being around you may conjure up the anxiety of having to communicate with them. Just the thought of people being around you may cause tightness in your throat even if you are alone when the thought occurs. Recognize the tension and be grateful that your body is effectively communicating with you. Then take a few minutes and breathe into the tension, allowing it to release with your exhalation. A new affirmation may arise from the tension that can help you with your first affirmation. In this example, you could use: "People enjoy being around me. I enjoy communicating with others."

Explore any resistant feelings that come up through the use of positive affirmations. These feelings are a result of our mental self criticism and our internal doubt (or NRs) and they can hamper the effectiveness of our affirmations.

Become conscious of all your thoughts, recognizing when you carry negative thoughts, doubts or fears. After you identify them, sit with them for a moment. It is important to examine the emotions that arise without judgment. Be sure you do not suppress any negative feelings you have. Allow them their time and space so that you can change them.

Do not repress your negative thoughts and feelings. That is like carpeting rotten floor boards. Pretty carpet won't look or smell pretty when it is continually exposed to something rotten. If you are angry, stressed, anxious or depressed, sugar coating those emotions won't do a thing for you except stand in the way of healing the deeper issues. Identify your thoughts and your emotions. Get to the root of the issue. Understand the past patterns you have had that allowed for that thought to arise. Recognize how that thinking served you in the past and how it no longer serves you. Then release it. After you've gone through this process, you can change your negative thoughts to positive ones. Gut the rotten floor board, build a new one and then lay down the pretty carpet.

Using a Mantra with Affirmations

A mantra is a repeated word or phrase that helps calm the mind for meditation. A mantra is a tool for reflection. It helps promote awareness. Sanskrit mantras have been around for thousands of years. They are natural sounds produced in the Universe. The most well known mantra is the word *aum* or *om* (ॐ). *Aum* is the beginning and end of sound. It is the vibration of the Universe that enables unlimited powers. It unites us with the Divine.

So hum is another mantra. It is Sanskrit for: "I am that" (which is so). More loosely translated, it is "I am all that I am" or "I am as I was created to be."

My favorite mantra is *Om Namaha Shivaya* (pronounced *aum na ma ha shee vy ya* or *aum na ma shee vy)*, which loosely translated from Sanskrit means: "I surrender to Spirit." I use this mantra all day long, especially when I want to be calmer, when I am cleaning and when I am walking or biking. I use it every time I am on an airplane during the take off and the landing. I use it when I am in traffic or waiting in line. It brings me serenity. It reminds me that there is a higher power that is always with me and whatever work I am doing is offered up to Spirit.

You can choose a mantra in English or in any other language. If your religious background is Christian, you may want a Latin mantra. If you were raised in a Jewish household, you may want a Hebrew mantra. Choose something with which you feel comfortable and will use throughout the day. If you feel comfortable with Sanskrit, I recommend you use *Om Namaha Shivaya*. It has been around for thousands of years and carries with it a powerful vibration.

After saying an affirmation, it is a great idea to repeat a mantra, which further avows your words. It calls your higher power to become part of the affirmation, reminding you that you aren't alone in making this change. The Universe will help make your affirmation a reality.

The Situations
(in alphabetical order by emotion)

ॐ When You're Being <u>A</u>bused

I choose to no longer be a victim. I am a strong and confident person. I deserve to have loving, peaceful people in my life. Only loving, peaceful people deserve to be in my life. Everyone in my world only wants what's best for me.

ॐ When You're <u>A</u>ccident Prone

I am coordinated and graceful. My body is safe and protected. I am innocent. I no longer need to hurt myself. (NOTE: Negative thoughts, focusing on the past or the future (not staying in the present) and forcing your will over the Universe can lead to physical pain.)

ॐ When You've Been (Falsely) <u>A</u>ccused

I am innocent. My innocence is recognized by the Universe and everything is resolved in its Divine time.

ॐ **When You're Feeling <u>A</u>ddicted (to someone, something)**

I am in control of my choices. I make choices that support my highest good and the highest good of others. I am ready to release old patterns that no longer serve me. Ultimate peace, love and happiness reside within me always. I can access these feelings all the time.

ॐ **When You're Feeling Taken <u>A</u>dvantage Of – See <u>U</u>sed**

ॐ **When You're Feeling <u>A</u>fraid – See Also <u>W</u>orried**

My intuition guides me through life safely. Everyone in my world only wants what's best for me. I welcome new people and experiences into my life with joy and trust. Releasing all fear allows the Universe's Divine plan for me to manifest. I am safe and protected.

ॐ **When You're Feeling <u>A</u>ggressive (in competition, the workplace...)**

I am at peace with the world around me. I can achieve my dreams and goals through controlled and rational ambition. I trust in the Universal timeline.

ॐ **When You're Feeling <u>A</u>ggressive (toward others)**

I am at peace with the world around me. I respect my needs and the needs of others. There is enough for everyone, including me. I fuel my aggression into finding ways in which everybody wins.

ॐ When You're Feeling <u>A</u>ngry

I breathe deeply and become calm before expressing my anger. I communicate my anger in a reasonable manner. I have a right to protect my boundaries. I have a right to express my anger in appropriate ways when my boundaries are threatened in inappropriate ways.

ॐ When You're <u>A</u>nnoyed

Everyone and everything in my world brings me peace and happiness. When I become annoyed by someone or something, I reflect upon what personal fears, issues and beliefs are causing me to be annoyed. I am grateful for others being a mirror for me and forcing me to recognize these issues.

ॐ When You're Feeling <u>A</u>nxious

I am calm at all times. I am safe at all times. I am protected at all times.

ॐ When You're Feeling <u>A</u>pathetic – See <u>I</u>ndifferent

ॐ When You're Feeling (Overly) <u>A</u>pologetic

I am perfect as I am now. I do not need to apologize for something I said with compassion before I know how it is received. I do not need to apologize for my talents, my good fortune or my good luck. I do not need to apologize for being unaware of something. I do not need to apologize for things outside of my power. I do not need to apologize for other people's unhappiness that they have created.

ॐ When You've Lost Your <u>A</u>ppetite

I am at peace. I am ready to listen to my body and its needs. I eat foods that are healthy and nourishing to my body and soul. I seek the perfect amount of food to keep my life force high.

ॐ When You're Feeling <u>A</u>rgumentative

I accept my beliefs as right for me today. I accept that other people's beliefs are right for them today. May every solution allow everybody to win.

ॐ When You're Feeling <u>A</u>rrogant – See <u>P</u>roud

ॐ When You're Feeling <u>A</u>shamed

I forgive myself for anything I have done in my past, whether it was intentional or unintentional. I forgive myself for anything that has happened to me. I release old patterns that led me to past situations of which I am not proud. I choose to release my shame and hold my head up high. I am a unique and Divine person.

ॐ When You're Unable to <u>A</u>sk Questions – See <u>R</u>eceive Help

🕉 **When You're Feeling Attached (to someone, something, an outcome)**

I release attachment. I embrace the Divine outcome the Universe has in store for me, free from all limitations of my mind and my current desire.

🕉 **When You're Feeling Awkward**

I am comfortable in my own skin. I am comfortable by myself and with others. I am confident and content. I enjoy expanding my comfort zone.

🕉 **When You're Feeling Bad-tempered**

Breathing deeply and calmly, I am ready to recognize what I have created in my life that has ignited my temper.

🕉 **When You Need to Bargain (in an unhealthy manner)**

It is not necessary to sacrifice or suffer in order to gain something. It is easy and effortless for all of my dreams and desires to be fulfilled.

🕉 **When You're Feeling Betrayed**

People love and support me. I only attract people in my world that want what is best for me.

ॐ When You're **B**laming Others

I control all of my thoughts and feelings. I make my own choices. I create my reality. I am therefore responsible for everything that happens to me. I create all the "good" and the "bad" in my life. No one is responsible for my happiness or my misery but me.

ॐ When You're Feeling **B**old/Blunt (to the point of offensiveness)

I have my own business to take care of, so I can ignore other people's business. I offer solicited, constructive criticism that comes from my heart. I speak with loving kindness.

ॐ When You're Feeling **B**ored

I create my reality. I control my own thoughts and perception. I have the power to change my reality at any given moment. I choose to live a life of excitement and awe.

ॐ When You're Feeling **B**rainwashed – See **M**anipulated

ॐ When You're Feeling **B**roke (financially) – See Also **L**acking (money)

I am grateful for all that has been given to me. I am open and receptive to receiving all that is being prepared for me that is for my highest good. The unlimited possibilities in the world make wealth inevitable for me.

ॐ When You're Feeling <u>B</u>roken (physically)

I am healthy, happy and whole.

ॐ When Things in Your Life are <u>B</u>roken

Everything in my care, including me, works perfectly.

ॐ When You're Feeling <u>C</u>antankerous – See <u>A</u>rgumentative & <u>B</u>ad-tempered

ॐ When You're Feeling <u>C</u>apricious

It is okay for me to change my mind. I allow myself time for decisions so that I can choose what is best for me and others.

ॐ When You're Feeling As If You're Being <u>C</u>hased

I am safe and protected at all times. I confront all that is sneaking up on me, whether it is real or imagined.

ॐ When You're Feeling As If You're <u>C</u>hasing (someone, something) – See Also <u>I</u>mpatient

Everything that is meant to happen to me manifests in its Divine time. I am neither too passive nor too aggressive in the pursuit of my dreams.

ॐ When You're Feeling Cheated/When You've Cheated

Everyone creates their reality and karma. I choose to forgive myself and others for any wrongs that have been committed. I ask others to forgive me if I have wronged them. May we now act in accordance with our higher selves.

ॐ When You're Feeling Close-Minded

I am open to the highest thought that is for the highest good.

ॐ When You're Feeling Cocky

I am confident in my abilities. I can focus on my talents without the need to earn anyone's recognition. I can appreciate the skills in myself and others.

ॐ When You're Unable to Commit

Knowing that nothing is guaranteed for eternity, I release the fear I have of commitment. When I am faced with a decision that requires a (long-term) commitment, I seek counsel from my heart and my higher power to help me make the right choice and feel comfortable with it. When something is right for me and everyone involved, I am able to commit to it. I commit fully to this moment and this day.

ॐ When You're Unable to Communicate

It is easy and effortless to communicate with others. My thoughts and feelings are important. I enjoy expressing myself. I embrace the power of my voice.

ॐ When You're Feeling Competitive

Knowing that we are all one, I want the best for me and the best for others. We are all made in the image of the Divine, therefore fighting others is only fighting myself and fighting the Universe. In my world, everybody wins.

ॐ When You're Feeling Complacent

I no longer remain in situations in my life that are less than ideal. I now choose to be in perfect situations. I deserve the best that life has to offer me.

ॐ When You're Complaining Often – See Also Negative

There are many wonderful things happening in my life and in the world around me. I focus on the "good" things in my life. When I focus on good, more good comes my way.

ॐ When You're Unable to Complete Something

If it is for my highest good, I can complete any task. I flow around obstacles that hinder completion. I ask for help and guidance when I need it, knowing that everything comes to fruition in a Divine timeline.

ॐ When You're Feeling That Life is Complicated

Everything I do is easy and effortless. Taking essential time-outs to breathe and meditate throughout the day help me to see things with clarity. Life is as simple as I now choose to make it.

ॐ When You're Unable to Give or Receive a Compliment

Recognizing the beautiful actions of others brings me bliss and adds to the beauty in the Universe. I enjoy giving and receiving heartfelt compliments.

ॐ When You're Unable to Concentrate – See Also Distracted & Unfocused

I become centered when I connect my body, mind and spirit with my breath.

ॐ When You're Lacking Confidence – See Also Doubt (Self-Doubt)

I always put my best effort into what I do. I am confident in my abilities.

ॐ When You're Conforming to Society (losing your individuality)

I am special and unique. The more I let the world see my unique qualities, the more others share their unique qualities. I choose what is best for me based on Divine guidance.

ॐ When You're Feeling <u>C</u>onfused – See Also <u>I</u>ndecisive

I believe in the Divine guidance of the Universe. Everything happens in its Divine time frame with its Divine purpose. With an open mind, I seek to understand the lessons from my experiences.

ॐ When You're Feeling (Too) <u>C</u>onservative

I accept new thoughts and ideas into my life. What is right for me now may be totally different from the way I was raised and that is okay. I embrace new ways of doing things.

ॐ When You're Feeling <u>C</u>onstrained – See <u>C</u>omplacent & <u>I</u>nhibited

ॐ When You're Feeling <u>C</u>ontrolled (by others) – See <u>M</u>anipulated

ॐ When You're <u>C</u>ontrolling (others) – See Also <u>M</u>anipulative

Being able to control my inhalation and exhalation and to create my entire reality are enough ways to exert my control in the Universe. I give others the space and freedom they need.

ॐ When You're Lacking <u>C</u>ourage

When I am led by the Universe, I have the confidence to do anything.

ॐ **When You're Feeling Crabby** – See **Bad-Tempered**

ॐ **When You're Craving (someone, something)** – See **Desire**

ॐ **When You're Feeling Critical** - See **Judgmental**

ॐ **When You're In Debt** – See **Lacking (money)**

ॐ **When You're Feeling Defeated**

I am a champion. I am a superstar. Everything I do is successful because I always do my best.

ॐ **When You're Feeling Defensive**

I always do my best. Other people respect and appreciate my thoughts and my work. My stamp of approval comes from the Universe.

ॐ **When You're Feeling Delusional**

I am clear about my Divine purpose. My connection to Spirit keeps me grounded in a lucid and present reality.

ॐ When You're in Denial

The truth is always revealed to me by my higher power.

ॐ When You're Unable to Depend on Others - See Trust Others

ॐ When You're Feeling Depressed

It is okay for me to express my feelings of anger, sadness and fear. I no longer need to wallow in these feelings. I trust in the present and the future. I trust in the good of human nature. I focus on the good in my life and the Universe. I am grateful for (list at least three things). Today, I choose to do at least one thing that brings me joy.

ॐ When You Desire (someone, something)

I have all that I need right now. I am safe and protected in this moment. I love and approve of myself. The unconditional love that the Universe has for me is all that I need. This unconditional love is stronger than anything else that I crave.

ॐ When You're Feeling Desperate – See Addicted & Desire

ॐ When You're Feeling Destructive – See Also Angry & Bad-tempered

I am at peace. I breathe deeply, releasing tension with every exhalation. Knowing that destruction does not solve any problem, I do not want to harm others, myself or any inanimate objects. I choose to solve my problems rationally, knowing that the perfect solution appears at the perfect time.

ॐ When You're Feeling Disapproval (from others)

I approve of myself. The Universe approves of me. It is not my business what others think of me. I release my judgment of others and they release their judgment of me.

ॐ When You're Disapproving (of others) – See Judgmental

ॐ When You're Feeling Disconnected (from the world)

Everyone and everything in the world is interrelated. There is a connection between all things. The life energy within me flows into others. I embrace the world around me. It is safe to let people into my world. It is safe for me to be connected to others.

ॐ When You're Feeling Disconnected (from your physical body)

Concentrating on my breath connects my mind, body and spirit. It is safe for me to be in my body. It is safe for me to experience the world around me.

ॐ When You're Discouraged – See Facing a Setback

ॐ When You're Feeling **D**isgusted

I am perfect as I am. Others are perfect as they are. Everything around me is in Divine order. I take action to make the necessary changes in my life when something isn't working for me.

ॐ When You're Feeling **D**ishonest

I now choose to act with integrity. I do what's best for everyone involved, including myself. I forgive myself for any past mistakes I've made.

ॐ When You're Feeling **D**isillusioned

I create my reality and am totally present in this reality. I detach from outcomes and flow with life. I detach from categories of "good" and "bad." I am ready to receive the universal abundance that is my birthright.

ॐ When You're Feeling **D**isinterested (in life) – See **C**omplacent

ॐ When You're Feeling **D**isloyal

My loyalty is unwavering because I make decisions with compassion for my highest good and the highest good of everyone concerned.

ॐ When You're Feeling **D**isorganized

Today I take action in my life to be more organized. I seek help from others to help me with my organization. I now choose to slow down my life to better plan and prepare.

ॐ When You're Feeling **D**issatisfied

I have the power to change my reality. I am grateful for all the good in my life.

ॐ When You're Feeling **D**istracted

By focusing inward on my breathing rhythm, I still my mind and my thoughts.

ॐ When You're Feeling the Need to **D**ominate – See **C**ontrolling

ॐ When You're in **D**oubt (about someone, something) – See **I**ndecisive

ॐ When You're in **D**oubt (Self-Doubt)

I can accomplish whatever I set my mind to. I am assisted by the Universe when I step toward my goals.

ॐ When You're Feeling <u>E</u>ffeminate/(Too) Feminine

My masculine and feminine sides are perfectly balanced. I am gentle and strong. I am patient and determined. I am nurturing and powerful.

ॐ When You're <u>E</u>mbarrassed

There are no mistakes. There are no stupid questions. When I find myself in situations that could be considered embarrassing, I learn to laugh rather than criticize myself. I act kindly toward others in potentially embarrassing situations, and they look kindly toward me.

ॐ When You're <u>E</u>nabling an Addiction

My actions serve myself and others for everyone's highest good. I choose to do only the things in my heart that feel right. I support myself and others by not enabling destructive behaviors.

ॐ When You're Feeling <u>E</u>nslaved

I create my reality and the situations within my reality. I deserve to lead the life I choose to lead. The Universe supports me when I choose to change my reality in a specific way that's for my highest good. I am always rewarded for the work I do. I deserve love and praise.

ॐ When You're Feeling <u>E</u>nvious - See <u>J</u>ealous

ॐ When You're Feeling <u>E</u>vil

I forgive myself for harboring any ill intent toward others. I see myself in others and recognize that any negative actions I commit are self-sabotaging.

ॐ When You're Unable to <u>E</u>xpress Yourself (creatively)

My creative energy and talents are ready to be expressed. It is safe to express myself in creative and nonconforming ways. When I express my creative side, I unlock the vault of creativity in the world around me.

ॐ When You're Unable to <u>E</u>xpress Yourself (emotionally)

It is safe for me to express my emotions. By expressing my emotions, I release the possibility of storing tension and pain in my body. There is great strength in shedding tears. There is great beauty in moving through emotions.

ॐ When You're Unable to <u>E</u>xpress Yourself (verbally)

My words are important to me and to others. Every time I speak my truth with compassion, I help others to speak their truth, too. Expressing my thoughts and feelings to others with good intent opens up channels of truth and light.

ॐ When You're Feeling as if You've <u>F</u>ailed – See Also Unable to <u>C</u>omplete & Facing a <u>S</u>etback

Every "failure" is a triumph. I see the lesson in everything I experience. My soul is enriched by my attempts in life regardless of the outcome. Something good comes from everything.

ॐ When You're Feeling as if You've Lost <u>F</u>aith – See <u>H</u>opeless

ॐ When You're Feeling <u>F</u>at – See <u>O</u>verweight

ॐ When You're <u>F</u>ighting (with someone)

Everyone wins when we choose the best solution for everyone involved. Knowing that we are all one, I want the best for me and the best for others. We are all made in the image of the Divine, therefore fighting others is only fighting myself and fighting the Universe.

ॐ When You're <u>F</u>ighting (with yourself)

I love myself and want to do everything that is in my best interest. When any part of me or my life is not at peace, I seek to find the root cause and restore harmony in my life. I can help others best when I am in harmony with myself.

ॐ When You're **F**orgetful

I am ready to deal with my past and my present. I am ready to remember the details of my life. I have an excellent memory.

ॐ When You're Unable to **F**orgive – See Also **R**esentment

Forgiving others brings me greater health and happiness. Forgiving others does not condone their behaviors, but instead it frees me from resentment and a victim mentality. I forgive _____ totally and completely. I move forward without ties binding me to past events or people.

ॐ When You're Feeling **F**rugal (with others)

The more I give, the more I receive. The more I help others to be prosperous, the more others help me to be prosperous. I enjoy fostering the goals and dreams of myself and others.

ॐ When You're Feeling **F**rugal (with yourself)

The more I give, the more I receive. I am a Divine being and I deserve to treat myself well. The more I give to myself, the more I give to others. I enjoy fostering the goals and dreams of myself and others.

ॐ **When You're Feeling Frustrated – See Also Impatient**

I trust that the perfect solution always arrives at the perfect time.

ॐ **When You're Feeling Frustrated (with affirmations)**

Positive affirmations work for me, whether or not I work with them. My positive frame of mind attracts positive people and situations to me.

ॐ **When You're Focused on the Future – See Not Staying Present**

ॐ **When You're Gaining Excessive Weight – See Also Overeating & Overweight**

I love myself and choose to nourish myself with high quality, healthy foods in the perfect amounts for me. I eat slowly and consciously. I exercise my body Divinely everyday.

ॐ **When You're Feeling Gluttonous – See Greedy**

ॐ When You Feel the Need to Gossip

My positive thoughts and words about others help the world become more harmonious. My self-esteem rises when I recognize the good in others and in myself. I release all judgment in myself and in others. If I have an issue with someone, I discuss it directly with him or her.

ॐ When You're Feeling Taken for Granted

I am loved and appreciated. I deserve recognition for my roles in life. I recognize the good I do in the world. The Universe recognizes the good I do in the world. Others recognize the good I do in the world.

ॐ When You're Feeling Greedy

I have all that I need in the moment. I am satisfied.

ॐ When You're Grieving (for a person, animal, end of a relationship)

I am grateful for all the special moments I've had with _____. The qualities I most enjoyed in _____ are _____ and _____. These qualities are present in my life in the following people or things: _____ and _____.

ॐ When You're Grieving (from a material loss)

I am grateful for the ways that I have been served by _____. I appreciate having had the opportunity to have had _____ in my life. May I now recognize the good that has come

out of this loss. I am grateful that I still have _____.
(Name three material items for which you are grateful.)

ॐ When You're Feeling Guilty

I forgive myself for past mistakes. I now choose to live
ethically and morally. I am the person I wish to see in the
world.

ॐ When You're Feeling Hardened – See Uncompassionate

ॐ When You're Feeling Hatred

My feelings add to the energy of the Universe. I choose to
radiate compassion to the world.

ॐ When You're Having Difficulty Hearing

I can hear clearly. I recognize and release issues from my
past that I did not want to hear. I now embrace the
beautiful sounds around me.

ॐ When You're Feeling Hesitant – See Also Indecisive

I make safe choices with ease and effortless effort. My
timing is beautiful.

ॐ When You're Feeling <u>H</u>opeless

I trust that the Universe has a Divine plan for me. When I take a step in the right direction on my path, opportunities appear.

ॐ When You're Feeling <u>I</u>gnored

I give myself an abundance of attention. Daily journaling gives me an outlet to express my thoughts and feelings so that they are always recognized. By giving others attention, I receive attention in return.

ॐ When You're Feeling <u>I</u>mmature

I am balanced between being playful and serious.

ॐ When You're Feeling <u>I</u>mpatient

I am grateful for all that has been prepared for me and all that is being prepared. I recognize that there is a perfect time for all events to unfold.

ॐ When You're Feeling <u>I</u>mpure

I am made in the image of the Divine, filled with pure light and love. Without shame or judgment, I recognize and release any thoughts or feelings that do not serve my highest good.

ॐ **When You're Feeling Incapable/Incompetent – See Doubt (Self-Doubt)**

ॐ **When You're Feeling Indecisive**

I always choose correctly when I release attachment and make decisions with my heart based on guidance from the Universe. With compassion and grace, I always make the right choice.

ॐ **When You're Feeling Indifferent**

I care about myself and make the best decisions for me and my environment. My opinion matters.

ॐ **When You're Feeling Infatuated – See Obsessed**

ॐ **When You're Feeling Inferior – See Insecure**

ॐ **When You're Feeling Inflexible**

I flow with the Universe and the Divine plan that has been set in motion for me. I flow with the continual changes in my life.

ॐ **When You're Feeling Inhibited**

I am safe to express myself. By freeing myself of my inhibitions, I free others of their inhibitions. When I expand my comfort zone, the Universe opens more doors for me.

ॐ When You're Feeling Insecure

I am safe and secure in every situation. I am comfortable in my body. Everyone is my equal. Everyone is unique and has special talents. I am grateful for being unique and enjoy sharing my special talents with others.

ॐ When You're Not Living in Integrity

My word is gold. I live by the highest standards of truth, simplicity and love and these high standards are reflected in my Universe.

ॐ When You're Interrupted (by others)

My words are important. With the compassion of my spirit and the power of my voice, I take command of the conversation. I enjoy listening to others and they enjoy listening to me.

ॐ When You're Interrupting (others)

I am a good listener. I enjoy listening to others and they enjoy listening to me.

ॐ When You're Afraid of Intimacy (personal)

It is safe for me to let others into my world. I release any past disappointment I have had with others.

ॐ When You're Afraid of Intimacy (sexual)

I am at ease with myself and my body. Verbalizing my fears to my partner, we can move at a comfortable pace. It is okay for me to stop or slow down when I need to. The right partner respects me for my honesty.

ॐ When You're Fighting Your Intuition

I trust that I am always led in the right direction. I choose to follow my intuition, knowing that the more I listen to it, the louder and more often it speaks.

ॐ When You're Feeling Invisible

I am a Divine individual. I recognize my Divinity. The Universe recognizes my Divinity. I make a positive impact in the world.

ॐ When You're Feeling Irresponsible

I deserve to enjoy myself at work and on my free time. My life is balanced between work and fun. I approach all tasks with an element of fun and joy. Bringing joy to myself and my environment makes me a responsible citizen.

ॐ When You're Feeling Irritable/Irritated

Breathing calmly and deeply, I find solace in the peace that is always present inside of me. I am grateful for anyone or anything that irritates me, bringing focus to these issues.

ॐ When You're Choosing to Isolate Yourself

I am outgoing. I enjoy meeting new people. I bring joy to others and they bring joy to me. It is safe to let people into my life.

ॐ When You're Feeling Isolated

It is easy and effortless for me to connect with others. People enjoy being around me. My personal magnetism is ever-increasing.

ॐ When You're Feeling Jaded – See Disillusioned

ॐ When You're Feeling Jealous

I am enough. I have enough. I do enough. I have all that I need and desire.

ॐ When You Dislike Your Job – See Also Complacent

I deserve to work in a job that I love. I deserve to be well compensated for my skills. I deserve to have fun while I'm working. I am ready to receive the perfect job for me.

ॐ **When You're Feeling Judgmental (of self or others)**

I recognize the Divine in everyone and everything. I am perfect just as I am. Others are perfect as they are.

-L-

ॐ **When You're Lacking (money)**

Money flows easily to me. People enjoy supporting me and I enjoy supporting them. I am ready to receive the abundance of the Universe. All my financial needs are met.

ॐ **When You're Lacking (self-esteem)**

I can accomplish anything. I am a champion. People adore me. My personal magnetism is strong and people love being around me.

ॐ **When You're Lacking (something)**

I am enough. I have enough. I do enough. I have everything I need in this moment.

ॐ **When You're Lacking (time) – See Also Overwhelmed**

I am in harmony with the Universe's schedule. I have all the time that I need to do all that I need to do.

ॐ When You're Lacking (willpower)

The Universe helps me with any resolution I make. When I feel my determination wavering, I step back from the situation and breathe deeply. My energy, life force and will increase with each breath. I ask for love and support from professionals and friends when I need it.

ॐ When You're Always Late

I allow myself plenty of time to prepare for things. I leave ten minutes early so that I can relax as I move toward my destination. My relaxed time schedule brings me great joy. I am in harmony with the schedule of the Universe.

ॐ When You're Feeling Lazy

My life is balanced between work and fun. I choose to make my work as enjoyable as my free time. I am motivated to increase my enjoyment in life. I have limitless joy and energy.

ॐ When You're Having Difficulty Learning

I learn in my own way, at my own speed. I understand things as I am able to process them. I am willing to do my best and to ask for help when I need it.

ॐ When You're Feeling Left out – See Isolated

ॐ When You're Feeling Lethargic – See Tired

ॐ When Your Libido is (Too) High

I love myself completely. I am at ease with my sexual energy, my sexual being and my body in this moment. I can displace my sexual energy to healthy physical energy or I can express my sexual energy in healthy sexual ways. Consensual sex is a natural and Divine activity. Sexual energy and spiritual energy help me express my love to others.

ॐ When Your Libido is Low

Sex is a natural and Divine activity. I love myself and my partner and express my love in sexual and nonsexual ways. I find things that make me feel sexy so that I can share that sexual feeling in a Divine way with my partner. I express my lack of sexual feelings openly with my partner, moving toward a resolution.

ॐ When You've Been Lied To

I deserve the truth. I can handle the truth. I am ready to confront those who have not been truthful with me. Everyone in my world enjoys telling the truth.

ॐ When You're Feeling Limited (by someone, something, yourself)

I live in a limitless reality. I created any limitations I have, real or imagined, and I now choose to dissolve them. I accept the abundance of the Universe. I am a magnet for all good things.

ॐ When You're Feeling **L**onely

I am lovable. People enjoy being around me. I am comfortable and content spending time alone and spending time with others. I am infinitely connected to everyone and everything in the Universe. I am never truly alone.

ॐ When You've Been Getting **L**ost

I ask for clear directions and clarify them before beginning my journey. When things seem uncertain, I verify directions with a third party. I am grateful to discover new places and new routes. It is easy to find my destination.

ॐ When You've **L**ost (an event)

I am a born champion. Whether I win or lose, knowing I have done my best is what's most important.

ॐ When You've **L**ost (something) – See **M**isplaced & **M**issing

ॐ When You're Withholding Giving or Receiving **L**ove

I gain courage and strength when I demonstrate my love for others and when I let others love me. I am now ready to share my love with the Universe. The Universe is ready to share its love with me.

ॐ When You're Feeling Lustful

I am complete as I am now. When the timing and situation is right, people come together in Divine ways. I am filled with the peace and love of the Universe, and I am willing to share that peace and love with others in a respectful, harmonious way.

ॐ When You're Lying (to yourself) – See Delusional & Denial

ॐ When You're Lying (to someone)

I speak my truth with confidence and compassion. People are grateful for my honesty.

ॐ When You're Feeling Manipulated

I am in control of my world. I control all of my thoughts and feelings. I make my own choices.

ॐ When You're Feeling Manipulative

I benefit most when others benefit, too. I respect everyone's free will.

ॐ When You're Feeling (Too) Masculine

My masculine and feminine sides are perfectly balanced. I am gentle and strong. I am patient and determined. I am nurturing and powerful.

ॐ When You're Feeling Masochistic

I am sweet and kind to myself first. I fill myself full of peace and love and share my abundance of peace and love to others. I love myself. I value myself.

ॐ When You're Feeling Materialistic

I have all that I need. The greatest things I possess are my health and happiness.

ॐ When You're Feeling Mean/Mean-Spirited

I recognize the good in myself and in others. I forgive myself and release any ill intent regarding others so that I can increase the good in the world.

ॐ When You're Feeling the Need to Always Mediate – (fix everything)

I allow others appropriate space to solve their issues. May the Highest thought prevail, allowing everyone to win.

ॐ When You've <u>M</u>isplaced Something

I can close my eyes and connect with the Universe to ask its guidance on where any particular object is at any particular time. When I become focused, answers quickly become clear to me.

ॐ When You're <u>M</u>issing (someone)

Any time I choose, I can call upon the beautiful memories I have of everyone who has a special place in my heart.

ॐ When You're <u>M</u>issing (something)

With patience and trust, everything returns to me in its right time and form. I accept that this form may change for the better.

ॐ When You're Feeling <u>M</u>isunderstood

The clearer I am about myself, the clearer others are about me. I understand myself. The Universe understands me. I can choose to verbally clarify anything that needs to be clarified to others.

ॐ When You're <u>M</u>oving Forward (with trepidation)

I am ready for my Divine purpose to manifest. I release the people, situations and things that no longer serve me. I accept into my life all that is for my highest good.

ॐ When You're Feeling <u>N</u>aïve

My connection to Infinite Intelligence makes me a sophisticated citizen of the Universe.

ॐ When You're Feeling <u>N</u>arcissistic

It is Divine and perfect to love myself. I am in balance with loving myself, loving others and loving the Universe. I satisfy my needs and the needs of others.

ॐ When You're Feeling <u>N</u>egative

My positive thoughts produce positive results. I alter my thoughts to produce the best reality for me and my world.

ॐ When You're Feeling <u>N</u>eglected (by others)

I recognize what I need to be content and I take care of these needs. Everyone in my world mirrors the positive way I treat myself.

ॐ When You're Feeling <u>N</u>eglected (by yourself)

I am a priority to me. I serve the world best with the energy I create when I take care of my needs.

ॐ When You're <u>N</u>eglecting (others)

I treat myself with loving kindness. I treat others with loving kindness.

ॐ When You're Feeling <u>N</u>ervous (before an event)

I am calm at all times. I am safe at all times. I always do my best.

ॐ When You're Feeling <u>N</u>ervous (in general) – See <u>A</u>nxious

ॐ When You're Having <u>N</u>ightmares

There are often "good" messages in "bad" dreams. By recording and analyzing my dreams, I acknowledge what my subconscious is telling me. I sleep safely and soundly, trusting inevitable resolutions for all the issues in my life.

ॐ When You're Feeling <u>N</u>on-Assertive – See <u>P</u>assive

ॐ When You're Withholding Giving or Receiving <u>N</u>urturing

I release the past resistance I have had toward nurturing. It is safe to be nurtured and to nurture others. I encourage the good in the Universe through nurturing myself and others. My inner child deserves to be nurtured.

ॐ When You're Feeling <u>O</u>bligated

Every activity I do is done best when I have joy in my heart. People want me to be with them with a sense of joy, not obligation. I honor others by choosing activities in which I want to participate, and by being honest with them when I am feeling obligated and not joyful.

ॐ When You're Feeling <u>O</u>bsessed

The Universe provides me with all I need and desire. I replace my obsession by trusting in the abundance of the Universe.

ॐ When You're Feeling <u>O</u>ld

I embrace my real age. I am always the perfect age for me. My body reacts beautifully to the loving care I give it. I eat Divinely. I exercise Divinely. I sleep Divinely. My cells are constantly regenerating, becoming whole and new. I rejuvenate my mind, body and spirit with youthful, fun activities that make me feel like a kid. I choose to have a functional age capacity of _____ years old.

ॐ When You're Feeling <u>O</u>ver-Ambitious

I take my time before agreeing to new commitments. I only take on new commitments that nourish my soul, bringing myself and others great joy. Through my intuition I recognize synchronistic events that support my Divine plan.

ॐ When You're Feeling Over-Committed

It is okay for me to release commitments that no longer serve my highest good. I take on only what I can handle, finding the perfect balance for my priorities. I choose to do nothing out of pure obligation.

ॐ When You're Overeating – See Also Addicted & Greedy

I choose to no longer eat to feel better about my problems. I do not need extra padding on my body to protect me from the world. I eat consciously and slowly, paying attention to my food so that I can fully receive its nourishment. I listen to my body, eating when I am hungry and stopping before I'm full.

ॐ When You're Feeling Overprotected (by someone) – See Smothered

ॐ When You're Being Overprotective (of someone)

I am able to remove myself from other people's business and allow them necessary time and space to grow.

ॐ When You're Being Overprotective (of something)

I enjoy having nice things and ideas to use for myself and to share with others. I enjoy other people sharing their things and ideas with me. Everything that has manifested on earth is here for the good of all when it is used ethically and responsibly.

ॐ When You're Feeling Overweight

I was made in the image of the Divine. I am beautiful. I have a beautiful body. I love and approve of myself. I approve of how much or how little I eat or exercise. I choose to eat healthfully and exercise my body Divinely every day.

ॐ When You're Feeling Overwhelmed

I recognize realistic time frames, maintaining a calm and peaceful schedule. I trust that I have all the time, energy and ability to accomplish all that I need to accomplish. I have clear priorities. I am ready to receive help to complete the necessary priorities in my life. I am able to communicate to others how they can help me.

-P-

ॐ When You're Feeling (Physical) Pain – See Also Appendix for specific healing affirmations

I seek to know the root cause of my pain and what my physical body is trying to tell me. I can release my physical illnesses by releasing my negative thoughts. I am ready to make the changes necessary in my life so that I may heal. I am no longer willing to carry pain in my body. I release all pain to the Universe. I think loving, conscious, positive thoughts. When I inhale, every cell in my body is enriched with Divine energy. (NOTE: Negative thoughts, focusing on the past or the future (not staying in the present) and forcing your will over the Universe can lead to physical pain.)

ॐ When You're Feeling <u>P</u>anicked – See <u>A</u>nxious

ॐ When You're Feeling <u>P</u>aranoid

I create a reality of serenity and privacy. I acknowledge who is allowed within my circle. I am safe within the protection of my world.

ॐ When You're Feeling (Too) <u>P</u>assive

The Universe assists me in manifesting my dreams and goals when I take the proper steps within my power to make them happen. The Universe provides me with opportunities, and it is up to me to act when these opportunities are provided. Three things I can do to make my dreams a reality today are: _____, _____ and _____.

ॐ When You're Not <u>P</u>aying Bills on Time – See Also <u>D</u>isorganized & <u>L</u>acking (money)

It is easy and fun to pay my bills on time. I enjoy paying people on time and others enjoy paying me on time. The more I give the more I receive. My payments multiply my wealth in unexpected ways.

ॐ When You're Feeling the Need to Be a <u>P</u>erfectionist

I am perfect as I am now.

ॐ When You're Feeling Perverse

I recognize that humans have a wide range of thoughts and emotions. I release my thoughts to my higher power. I respect others as Divine beings. I respect myself as a Divine being.

ॐ When You're Feeling Poor – See Lacking (money)

ॐ When You're Feeling Power Hungry – See Also Controlling & Manipulative

I have the power to create my reality. I have infinite power through my connection to the Universe. My power comes from within, rather than being based on my control over others or external situations.

ॐ When You're Feeling Powerless – See Also Manipulated

Inside me, there is boundless strength and tenacity. I have limitless power.

ॐ When You're Not Staying Present

I am here in this moment, safe and protected. All is well in my world right now. Maintaining my focus on my breath keeps me focused on the present moment.

ॐ When You're Having <u>P</u>roblems (with authority)

I regard the spirit of the law for the highest good of everyone.

ॐ When You're Having <u>P</u>roblems (with children, pets in your care)

Children and pets are mirrors of their environment. When I am in harmony with my environment, everyone in my environment is in harmony with me.

ॐ When You're Feeling <u>P</u>roud

I feel good about myself without needing attention from others. I am grateful for my talents and generously share them with others. I release my ego.

ॐ When You're Feeling <u>R</u>ebellious

The choices I make are for the highest good of everyone involved. I make safe and responsible choices.

ॐ When You're Unable to <u>R</u>eceive Help

I enjoy helping others and they enjoy helping me. By giving someone an opportunity to help me, I increase their self-esteem, helping them to feel useful and needed.

ॐ **When You're Feeling Regretful – See Remorseful**

ॐ **When You're Afraid of Rejection**

I gain strength and perseverance through my attempts in life. When one door closes, another one opens.

ॐ **When You're Unable to Relax**

I still my mind and my thoughts, concentrating on my inhale and exhale. With each exhale, I feel my body soften and relax. Each exhale helps me to release. Each exhale helps me to let go. Each exhale helps me to surrender. When I allow myself time to relax, I am freeing myself to be more efficient and productive.

ॐ **When You're Unable to Release (someone, something)**

When someone or something leaves me, space is cleared for someone or something better suited to me.

ॐ **When You're Having Trouble Remembering – See Forgetful**

ॐ **When You're Feeling Remorseful**

All the decisions I have made have helped me to become the person I am today. I forgive myself for any decisions I now regret. I have learned valuable lessons from my decisions.

ॐ When You're Harboring Resentment

Knowing that it does not serve me in any way to harbor resentment, I send out peace and love to everyone. I understand that people enter my world so that I can learn from them. Help me to see the lesson. I choose to recognize and heal my resentment by releasing it and replacing it with gratitude. By releasing my resentment, I now allow abundance to come to me.

ॐ When You're Feeling Resistant (to something positive) – See Also Moving Forward

I recognize what is beneficial to me. I get quality sleep, food and exercise. I get great pleasure from maintaining good health and a life free of stress. I embrace positive new changes that are for my highest good.

ॐ When You're Feeling Restless

I do enough. I am comfortable in my body right now. My life is peaceful. I follow my intuition when contemplating adding to my life.

ॐ When You're Feeling Rude

My thoughts, words and actions radiate compassion.

ॐ When You're Feeling As Though You Need to <u>R</u>un Away

I release the pain of my past. I embrace the unknown of the future. I bask in the safety of this moment. I can handle any situation that I face with the power that dwells in me.

ॐ When You're Feeling As Though You're <u>R</u>unning in Circles

Breathing and meditating help me to become clear and focused. When I get sidetracked from my path, I check in with my higher power to help me get back on track.

ॐ When You're Feeling <u>S</u>ad – See <u>D</u>epressed

ॐ When You're Feeling <u>S</u>adistic – See <u>M</u>ean/Mean-Spirited

ॐ When You're Feeling <u>S</u>cared – See <u>A</u>fraid

ॐ When You're Having Difficulty <u>S</u>eeing (the big picture)

I can see the big picture and the bottom line. I am able to see the consequences of my actions. My vision is balanced between fine details and final results.

ॐ When You're Having Difficulty <u>S</u>eeing (the details)

I am ready to see the details of my past, present and future. I revel in the beautiful details around me, such as the smell of the rain, the warmth of the sun, the leaves rustling in the wind, the shape of the clouds and the dance of the squirrels. My vision is balanced between fine details and final results.

ॐ When You're Having Difficulty <u>S</u>eeing (physically)

I can see clearly. I am ready to see the details of my past, present and future. I release any tension that may be affecting my eyesight. My eyes are now able to witness the beauty in the Universe.

ॐ When You're Feeling <u>S</u>elf Conscious – See <u>D</u>isapproval

ॐ When You're Feeling <u>S</u>elfish

My focus is to be in harmony with the Universe. I release issues that focus solely on me, especially regarding attachment and desire. My life is balanced between taking care of my needs and taking care of others.

ॐ When You're Feeling <u>S</u>elf-Hatred

I love myself. I am lovable. I accept and approve of myself. I deserve an infinite wealth of nurturing and compassion. The more I love and approve of myself, the more others love and approve of themselves. I am Divine.

ॐ When You're Feeling <u>S</u>elf-Important

Everyone is equally important in the presence of the Divine.

ॐ When You're Feeling <u>S</u>elf-Pity

I am lovable. People enjoy being around me. I release any person, thought or situation which is no longer serving me. I have created a beautiful reality. My world is filled with everything good. I am happy, healthy and whole. I am grateful for (list at least three things).

ॐ When You're Feeling <u>S</u>ensitive

I allow my emotions to flow freely. Knowing that everyone carries emotional baggage, I do not take things personally.

ॐ When You're <u>S</u>eparated (from someone, something) – See <u>M</u>isplaced & <u>M</u>issing

ॐ When You're Feeling (Too) <u>S</u>erious

Life is a fun and exciting game. I am always a winner and so is everyone playing with me. The more fun I can give and receive in the game, the more all of us win.

ॐ **When You're Facing a Setback – See Also Unable to Complete Something**

Setbacks are a natural and positive key to change. I trust in the process of this setback, knowing I now have an opportunity to approach this situation differently and better.

ॐ **When You're Feeling Shallow**

There is a depth to my soul recognized by my highest self. I release my self concern and my trivial concerns. I focus on fulfilling my Divine plan in the Universe.

ॐ **When You're Having Difficulty Sharing**

I see myself in others. I embrace the opportunity to share what I am able and willing to share. I take care of others with compassion, just as I enjoy being taken care of. I enjoy receiving what others share with me.

ॐ **When You're Feeling Short (of breath)**

I am calm. I am relaxed. I am connected to an infinite source of breath and life. I choose to breathe freely and fully. I am loved. I am safe at all times.

ॐ **When You're Feeling Short (in stature)**

I am the perfect height for me.

ॐ When You're Feeling <u>S</u>hort (with others)

I am patient and kind. I relax and listen to others when they are speaking, giving them my full attention. I speak using necessary detail.

ॐ When You're Feeling <u>S</u>hy

Expressing my thoughts and feelings to others with compassion opens up channels of truth and light. I am comfortable in the presence of others.

ॐ When You're Feeling <u>S</u>ick – See Physical <u>P</u>ain & Appendix

ॐ When You're Having Difficulty <u>S</u>leeping – See Also <u>N</u>ightmares

I release all of my stress before I get into bed, allowing only peaceful energy to sleep with me. I now focus on the word "peace" on my inhalation and the word "love" on my exhalation. When thoughts enter my mind, I return my focus to "peace" and "love," "peace" and "love," "peace" and "love."

ॐ When You're Having Difficulty <u>S</u>melling

My sense of smell is keen. I recognize and release what has limited my sense of smell in the past. I can inhale the full essence of all the scents in the world.

ॐ When You're Feeling <u>S</u>mothered

I recognize when I need time and space for myself. I ask others to give me the time and space I need. I can always find inner space and solitude even when external distractions surround me.

ॐ When You're Feeling <u>S</u>orry For Yourself – See <u>S</u>elf-Pity

ॐ When You're Having Difficulty <u>S</u>peaking - See <u>E</u>xpress Yourself (verbally)

ॐ When You're Unable to Get <u>S</u>tarted – See Also <u>U</u>nmotivated

I release my former pattern of struggle. Everything is easy with the support of the Universe. I trust that as I step in the right direction, my path appears.

ॐ When You're <u>S</u>tarting Over

Every time I start something new, my life urge becomes stronger. Starting over helps me approach a situation from a different direction. It provides me the opportunity to meet new people and have new experiences.

ॐ When You've <u>S</u>tolen

I forgive myself for having stolen. In whatever way possible, I will do my best to remedy the situation. If I cannot "payback" what I have stolen, I will find a way to "pay it forward" to someone else.

ॐ When You've Had Something <u>S</u>tolen From You

I forgive whoever has stolen from me. I deserve all that I have and I desire to keep all that I have until I choose to release it. I choose to strengthen my trust in human nature by focusing on the good things that are present in my life.

ॐ When You're Feeling <u>S</u>tressed

I breathe deeply and become calm. I believe all that happens to me results in good. I trust that I have all the time, energy and ability to accomplish all that I need to do.

ॐ When You're <u>S</u>truggling

I release the negative thoughts that I am holding which are keeping me in a pattern of struggling. I now accept an easy and effortless life. I allow pleasure to come into all areas of my life.

ॐ When You're Feeling <u>S</u>tuck (in a commitment, situation...)

It is safe and important for me to honor my will and release commitments that no longer serve my highest good. It is safe for me to be honest with other people about my feelings.

ॐ When You're Feeling <u>S</u>tuck (in old patterns) – See Also <u>M</u>oving Forward

I am ready to recognize and release what no longer serves my highest good. I am ready to release old limitations. I am ready to embrace healthy new changes.

ॐ When You're <u>S</u>tuck (in the past) – See Not Staying <u>P</u>resent

ॐ When You're Feeling <u>S</u>tupid

It is okay to be a novice. I do not need to be a master in everything, although I can master anything I wish to master. I appreciate others who are already experts in certain fields. I can learn from them and ask them for help. I have intelligence about topics that interest me.

ॐ When You're Feeling as though you're <u>S</u>uffocating – See <u>S</u>mothered

ॐ When You're Feeling <u>S</u>uicidal – See Also <u>D</u>epressed

I continue to turn corners in my life with faith and trust, knowing that golden opportunities surround me when I am open to receiving them. I ask for love and support from professionals and friends when I need it.

ॐ When You're Feeling <u>S</u>uperior to Others

We are all made of Universal energy and spirit. Everyone is my equal. I am neither above nor beneath anyone.

ॐ When You're Feeling (Too) <u>T</u>alkative

I am grateful for the ability to be outgoing. I now embrace the opportunity to be silent and still. I am comfortable with silence. Being silent gives me an opportunity to learn from others and from my higher power.

ॐ When You're Being <u>T</u>eased

I deserve to be treated with loving kindness by everyone. Everyone in my world respects me.

ॐ When You're Feeling <u>T</u>hreatened – See <u>M</u>anipulated

ॐ When You're Feeling <u>T</u>ired

The Universe always provides me with abundant energy. I can tap into the Universe's infinite source of energy anytime I need it.

ॐ When You're Feeling <u>T</u>rapped – See <u>C</u>omplacent

ॐ When You're Unable to <u>T</u>rust (others)

I release whatever need I had for people to lie to me in the past. Everyone in my world now tells me the truth.   It is safe to put my trust in others and in myself. Others put their trust in me.

ॐ When You're Unable to **T**rust (yourself)

I am filled with integrity. My word is gold.

ॐ When You're Feeling **U**gly

I was made in the image of the Divine. I am beautiful. I love and approve of myself always.

ॐ When You're Feeling **U**nappreciated – See Also Taken for **G**ranted

I express my appreciation of others. I acknowledge the appreciation I have for myself and my world. I appreciate all that I do for myself and all that I do for others. I know that I make a positive difference in the world.

ॐ When You're Feeling **U**nappreciative – See **U**ngrateful

ॐ When You're Feeling **U**nbalanced

I am strong and stable. I can easily balance my physical energy body with earth, air, water or fire by spending time outdoors, breathing fresh air, sitting alone by a fire, swimming or bathing. I breathe deeply into my core where I am centered and strong.

ॐ When You're Feeling <u>U</u>ncomfortable in Your Skin

The more comfortable I am in my skin, the more at ease others are around me. I wear comfortable clothes. I maintain a comfortable temperature. I relax in my body. I am at peace in my body.

ॐ When You're Feeling <u>U</u>ncompassionate

Knowing that my neighbors are an extension of myself and that we are all in this world together, I reach out to them with compassion and love.

ॐ When You're Feeling <u>U</u>nconnected

The energy of the Universe is unbounded. I am part of this energy. My family and friends are part of this energy. My neighbors are part of this energy. I am connected to everything that exists. Everything that exists is connected to me.

ॐ When You're Feeling <u>U</u>ncooperative

Since we are all made of Divine energy, sharing with others is like sharing with myself. I embrace the support of others and they embrace my support.

ॐ When You're Feeling Underlined Uncreative

I am open and ready to receive Divine inspiration. I am ready for my creativity to bloom. My creative energy and talents are ready to be expressed. I now create the time and space to allow this expression. I devote a portion of my day for my creative pursuits.

ॐ When You're Feeling Unfocused

Breathing and meditating help me to become clear and focused. I know that I can always find inner peace and solitude no matter what external distractions surround me. When something is weighing heavily on me, I choose to process through it for clarity and healing.

ॐ When You're Feeling Ungrateful

Every green light, every blade of grass and every breath is a gift to me. I appreciate everything, no matter how small, "good" or "bad." I am grateful for everything that I have received and everything that is being prepared for me. I am grateful for the people in my life. I am grateful for: _____ (list ten things/people).

ॐ When You're Unhappy with Someone's Decision (for herself/himself)

I find happiness within myself. I approve of myself. It is not my business to approve what other people do. I speak with truth and compassion when my words can help others.

ॐ When You're Unhappy with Someone's Decision (involving you)

I create my reality. I have influence in every decision that is made regarding me. I now embrace my reality or take action to alter it as necessary.

ॐ When You're Making Unhealthy Choices - See Also Addicted

I appreciate a high quality of life. I become conscious of my thoughts and actions. I now choose to live well. I honor my body with perfect amounts of food, sleep and exercise.

ॐ When You're Feeling Unimportant - See Also Unappreciated

Everyone, including me, plays a unique and vital role in the lives of others.

ॐ When You're Feeling Unlovable

I am lovable. People enjoy being around me.

ॐ When You're Feeling Unlucky

I am blessed. Good things come to me easily and effortlessly. When I flow with the Universe, luck naturally gravitates to me. Golden opportunities surround me.

ॐ When You're Feeling <u>U</u>nmotivated

I can accomplish anything I set my mind to. I release my resistance, knowing that everything can be easy when I have the support of the Universe.

ॐ When You're Feeling <u>U</u>nsuccessful

I am successful because I make a positive difference in the world. Every person I help in some way, no matter how small, makes me a success. Every smile I witness on myself or others adds to my success.

ॐ When You're Feeling <u>U</u>nsupported

I am always loved. I am always taken care of. I feel the love and support around me at all times.

ॐ When You're Feeling <u>U</u>ptight – See Unable to <u>R</u>elax

ॐ When You're Feeling <u>U</u>sed

People appreciate and respect me. I am valued for being me.

ॐ When You're Feeling <u>U</u>seless

I am willing to help others. I make the world a better place through my love and generosity to others. Today I have helped others by _____. (Name three ways you helped people today. If you can't, think of three ways you can help others tomorrow and DO them!)

ॐ When You're Feeling <u>V</u>ain

It is okay for me to be a priority to myself. It is okay for me to be a priority to others. My ultimate priority is to fulfill my Divine purpose.

ॐ When You're Feeling <u>V</u>engeful

I choose to resolve and release past issues and harness my energy toward good. The more good I cast out, the more good I reel in.

ॐ When You're Feeling <u>V</u>ictimized – See <u>A</u>bused

ॐ When You're Feeling <u>V</u>ulnerable

I own my thoughts and feelings. I am safe in the present moment. It is safe to open myself up to new people and new experiences that radiate Divine energy. I am safe in my vulnerability.

ॐ **When You <u>W</u>ant (attention) – See <u>I</u>gnored**

ॐ **When You <u>W</u>ant (someone, something) – See <u>D</u>esire**

ॐ **When You're Feeling Like You're <u>W</u>asting (time)**

My time is well spent when I'm increasing the good in the world.

ॐ **When You're Feeling Like You're <u>W</u>asting (energy, food, talents…)**

When I act from a place of awareness and compassion, everything I do and everything I use is beneficial to the greater good of the Universe.

ॐ **When You're Feeling Like You're <u>W</u>asting (money)**

I enjoy spending money that increases the peace, harmony and beauty in the world.

ॐ **When You're Feeling <u>W</u>eak**

My connection to the Universe always provides me with an abundance of strength and energy. There is strength in my breath and in my body. As long as I have the power to breathe, I have the power to create my reality and the strength that I need within that reality.

ॐ When You're <u>W</u>orried

All is right in my world. I am safe at all times. Everyone I know is safe and protected. Every solution arrives in its own time. I (release all doubt and) put my faith in the Universe.

ॐ When You're <u>W</u>orried (about what others think) – See <u>D</u>isapproval

ॐ When You're Feeling <u>W</u>orthless – See <u>U</u>seless

ॐ When You're Feeling Like You're Always <u>W</u>rong

I am perfect and Divine. Everything I do is perfect for me.

ॐ When You're Feeling (Too) <u>Y</u>oung

I am mature, responsible and patient. Everyday, I gain valuable life experience. I trust that all good things will come to me in a Divine timeline. I embrace my real age. I am always the perfect age for me.

Appendix - Healing Affirmations for the Physical Body based on the Chakras

The affirmations in this section are categorized by the seven energy centers in the body, called chakras. (See the following page for a detailed picture of the basic locations of the seven chakras.) Each chakra contains certain parts of the body within that region. Correlate the location of your physical pain with the appropriate chakra. Read the healing affirmations for that chakra. If there are several categories, pick which one is most applicable for you right now. For example, if I am having lower back pain, I would look at the navel chakra for my affirmations. Lower back pain often comes with a feeling of not being supported. The money affirmations are appropriate for me if I feel unsupported financially. The sexuality/relationships affirmations are appropriate for me if I feel I'm in an unsupported relationship. The creativity affirmations are appropriate for me if I am not honoring my creative abilities or devoting time to them.

This is not a complete guide of healing affirmations for the physical body, but it is a great initial reference. These affirmations work nicely in conjunction with holistic healing and/or western medicine. As always, with any affirmations, feel free to mold and adapt this to best suit your needs.

Chart of the Chakras

~ Chakras ~
Seven Energy Centers in the Body

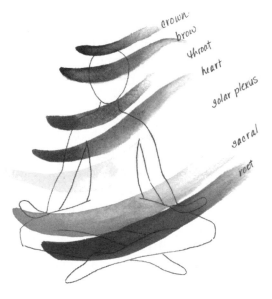

crown
brow
throat
heart
solar plexus
sacral
root

Chakra 1 – The Root Chakra –

Located at the base of the spine, it involves the immune system, kidneys, rectum, spinal column, legs, feet and bones. It is associated with the color red.

Acceptance

I am lovable. I love myself totally and completely. I accept and approve of myself totally and completely. I am made in the image of the Divine. I deserve an infinite wealth of nurturing and compassion. I accept myself and the world around me. Everyone accepts me for who I am and what I stand for. It is okay for me to have different beliefs than my family. It is okay for others to have different beliefs than me. I am grounded and centered with the earth. I am successful. I accept new thoughts and ideas into my life. I embrace new ways of doing things. I am always protected and nurtured. People only want what's best for me. All is right in my world. We are all one.

Chakra 2 – The Sacral Chakra –

Located between the lower abdomen to the navel, it involves the ovaries, testicles, prostrate, genitals, womb, appendix, pelvis and bladder. It is associated with the color orange.

Creativity

I am creative. I am open and ready to receive Divine inspiration. I devote a portion of my day for my creative pursuits. I am a channel for Divine creativity. I am ready for my creativity to bloom. It is easy to express my creative energy and talents. I now create the time and space to allow this expression.

Relationships/Sexuality

I displace my sexual energy to healthy physical energy or I can express my sexual energy in sexual ways. I am at ease with my sexual energy, my sexual being and my body in this moment. Sex is a natural and Divine activity. Sexual energy and spiritual energy both help me express my love. I release any disappointment I have had with others. It is now safe for me to let others into my world. I am safe in my vulnerability. Verbalizing my fears to my partner, we move at a comfortable pace. It is okay for me to stop or slow down when I need to. The right partner always respects me for my honesty. I recognize when I need time and space for myself. I ask others to allow me this freedom. I always find inner space and solitude in any environment. I am able to remove myself from other people's business and allow them necessary time and space to grow.

Money

Money flows easily to me. People enjoy supporting me. I enjoy supporting worthy endeavors. I am ready to receive the abundance of the Universe. All my financial needs are met. The more I give, the more I receive. I am made in the image of the Divine and I deserve to treat myself well. The more I help others prosper, the more others help me prosper. My wealth multiplies in unexpected ways. I work in a job that I love, surrounded by people who love and support me and whom I love and support. I am well compensated for my skills in the most appropriate work environment for me.

Chakra 3 – The Solar Plexus Chakra –

Located between the navel and the chest, it involves the pancreas, adrenals, stomach, intestines, liver, spleen, gall bladder, kidneys, nervous system. It is associated with the color yellow.

Determination/Commitment

The Universe helps me with any resolution I make. When I feel my determination wavering, I step back from the situation and breathe deeply. I ask for love and support from professionals and friends when I need it. I can accomplish anything I set my mind to. I trust that I have all the time, energy and ability to accomplish all that I need to accomplish. Knowing that nothing is guaranteed for eternity, I release the fear I have of commitment. When I am faced with a decision that requires a (long-term) commitment, I always make the right choice and feel comfortable with it. When something is right for me and everyone involved, I am able to commit to it.

Energy

The Universe always provides me with abundant energy. I can tap into the Universe's infinite source of energy anytime I need it.

Body Mastery

I am strong and stable. I easily balance my physical energy body with earth, air, water or fire by spending time outdoors, breathing fresh air, sitting alone by a fire, swimming or bathing. I breathe deeply and reach into my core where I am centered and strong. Everything in my world comes into balance from this place. I was made in the image of the Divine. Knowing that I was made in the image of the Divine, I now choose to eat healthfully. I exercise my body Divinely. I am beautiful at any size or shape. I am the perfect size and shape for me. I am the perfect height for me. I love and approve of myself no matter how much or how little I eat or exercise. My cells are constantly regenerating, becoming whole and new. I rejuvenate my mind, body and spirit with youthful, fun activities that make me feel like a kid. I choose to have a functional age capacity of ____ years old. I am the perfect age for me.

Chakra 4 – The Heart Chakra –

Located at the center of the chest, it involves the heart and the rest of the circulatory system, lungs, diaphragm, thymus gland, ribs, breasts, shoulders, arms and hands. It is associated with the color green.

Love/Compassion

Knowing that my neighbors are an extension of myself and that we are all in this world together, I reach out to them with compassion and love. All the energy in the Universe is interrelated. I am part of this energy. My friends and family are part of this energy. My neighbors are part of this energy. I always find the connection I'm looking for if it is for my highest good. I recognize the Divine in everyone and everything. I am perfect as I am now. Others are perfect as they are now. I radiate compassion to everyone (no matter what feelings they return toward me). Knowing that we are all one, I want the best for me and the best for others. We are all made in the image of the Divine, therefore fighting others is only fighting myself and ultimately fighting my higher power. There is enough for everyone.

Forgiveness

Knowing that it does not serve me in any way to harbor resentment, I send out peace and love to everyone. I understand that people enter my world so that I can learn from them. Forgiving others brings me greater health and happiness. It does not condone their behaviors, but instead it frees me from resentment and a victim mentality. I move forward without ties binding me to past events or people.

Gratitude

Every green light, every blade of grass and every breath I take is a great gift to me. I appreciate everything, no matter how small, "good" or "bad." I am grateful for everything I have received and everything that is being prepared for me. I am grateful for all the people in my life. Today, I am especially grateful for: _____
(list ten things or people).

Anger/Betrayal/Loneliness

I breathe deeply and become calm before expressing my anger. I communicate my anger in a reasonable manner. I have a right to protect my boundaries. I have a right to express my anger in appropriate ways when my boundaries are threatened in inappropriate ways. People love and support me. I only attract people in my world that want what's best for me. I am lovable. People enjoy being around me. I am comfortable and content spending time alone or spending time with other people. I am infinitely connected to everything and everyone in the Universe. I am never truly alone.

Chakra 5 — The Throat Chakra —

Located at the throat, it involves the thyroid, parathyroid, hypothalamus, esophagus, throat and mouth. It is associated with the color blue.

Communication/Expression

My thoughts and feelings are important. I have a right to express myself when it is for the highest good of others. My words are important to me and to others. My creative energy and talents are ready to be expressed. It is safe to express myself in creative and nonconforming ways. Every time I speak my truth, I help others to speak their truth, too. Expressing my thoughts and feelings to others with compassion opens up channels of truth and light.

Will/Desire

Every activity I do is done best when I have joy in my heart. Others want me to be with them with a sense of joy, not obligation. I honor others by choosing activities in which I want to participate, and by being honest with them when I am feeling obligated.

Chakra 6 – The Brow Chakra –

Located at the center of the forehead, between the eyebrows at the third eye, it involves the pituitary gland, pineal gland, the left eye, nose and ears. It is associated with the color indigo.

Clarity/Consciousness/Intuition

I am always led in the right direction. I listen to my intuition and follow my inner voice. The more I listen to my intuition, the louder and more often it speaks.

Chakra 7 – The Crown Chakra –

Located at the top of the head, it involves the cerebral cortex, central nervous system, muscular system, skeletal system, skin and the right eye. It is associated with the color purple.

Connection with the Divine

The energy of the Universe is interrelated. I am part of this energy. I always find the connection I'm looking for that is for my highest good. I am made in the image of the Divine. I have a Divine connection with infinite wisdom. Based on my spiritual bloodline, I have the genetics of a super star.

May your journey be filled
In Truth, Simplicity and Love
Om Namaha Shivaya

Deanna Reiter teaches workshops, seminars and retreats around the world. She welcomes feedback about *Dancing with Divinity*. Please write Deanna with your personal stories using the affirmations in this book. If there is a category that you feel should be included in a second edition of *Dancing with Divinity*, e-mail Deanna through her website:

The Dayawati Center

Center for Compassion & Spiritual Connection

www.dayawati.com

Coming in 2008...

Ultimate Joy

Discover the joy that leaves you content knowing there is nothing you would rather be doing than what you are doing each and every moment, fully present in the world with a smile on your face. Create the joy in your life that allows you to wake up refreshed, excited and energetic about the day ahead. It is this joy that you can possess; you only need to access it. *Ultimate Joy* is the key to your contentment.

Dancing with Divinity
Compact Disc

All musical compositions composed, arranged and performed by
Rahjta Ren

Total 64:02
1. Dancing With Divinity 1:58 Deanna Reiter, Hanakia Zedek
2. Introduction 6:58 Deanna Reiter
3. The Five Treasures: I & II 10:58 Deanna Reiter, Hanakia Zedek
4. The Five Treasures: III 3:57 Hanakia Zedek
5. The Five Treasures: IV 4:43 Deanna Reiter
6. The Five Treasures: V 3:54 Deanna Reiter, Hanakia Zedek
7. Relaxing Into Safety 4:14 Susan Shehata
8. Compassion 3:25 Pam Nelson
9. Joy 1:45 Dave Nelson
10. Self Acceptance 3:41 Dr. Rory Flaherty
11. Communication 3:29 Deanna Reiter
12. Creativity And Wealth 4:39 Rahjta Ren
13. Success 5:55 Colleen Buckman
14. Personal Reality 3:53 Hanakia Zedek

Manufactured by Copycats Media, Minneapolis, Minnesota
Recorded, mixed and mastered at Ren's Den , Minneapolis, Minnesota
Copyright Rahjta Ren, 2007

All compositions Natural Order Music Publishing, BMI